MIDI TOUCH MUSICAL INSTRUMENTS USING THE ARDUINO

TOM SCARFF

TABLE OF CONTENTS

Figures

Pictures

Listings

Tables

PREFACE

This book contains designs for MIDI Touch Musical Instruments using the Arduino hardware and software.

An Introduction to MIDI Touch Musical Instruments

The MIDI Touch Interface uses a technology called capacitive sensing. The MIDI Touch board measures the capacitance of the objects connected to the inputs. Once you touch, or come close to the object, it can sense the additional capacitance added from the human body, which then triggers a note.

It works with anything that is electrically conductive, so it has to be a material that allows electricity to flow through it, such as aluminium foil and metal objects. However, the material only has to be slightly conductive, so plants, fruit, flowers, vegetables and water can also work!

Also because it uses capacitive sensing the conductive materials used can be triggered through thin non-conductive material such as paper or glass. This means you can print out shapes onto paper and then stick metal foil to the back of the paper to create all sorts of musical instruments.

Designing and building your own MIDI Touch controller using Capacitive Sensing Technology can provide you with a product that matches your exact requirements. Playability, functionality, portability, connectivity and expense are just some of the design considerations.

1.1 What is Body Capacitance?

Body capacitance refers to the physical property of the human body that has it act as a capacitor. Like any other electrically-conductive object, a human body can store electric charge if insulated.

The Capacitance of a human body in normal surroundings is typically in the tens to low hundreds of pico-Farads (pF). While humans are much larger than typical electronic components, they are also mostly separated by significant distance from other conductive objects. Although the occasional static shock can be startling and unpleasant, the amount of stored energy is relatively low. The Human Body Model for capacitance, as defined by the Electrostatic Discharge Association (ESDA) is a 100pF capacitor in series with a 1500 ohm (1.5kΩ) resistor.

Finger capacitance is the colloquial term used to describe the electrical charge added to a capacitance touch switch surface in respond to a touch command. When you place your finger on the surface of a capacitance touch switch it will absorb some of your body's electrical charge. It is a small electrical charge that only the capacitance touch switch will notice.

1.2 What is a MIDI Touch Controller Interface?

With a MIDI Touch Controller Interface board you can make music from anything conductive, whether you are a musician creating new ways of interacting with sound, or exploring music and electronics for the first time.

The designs in this book allow you to connect the MIDI Touch Interface board to a computer using a standard USB cable or the standard MIDI 5-Pin DIN socket.

A MIDI controller usually consists of a small keyboard, potentiometers, sliders, switches, buttons, foot pedals and sensors which can be converted into various MIDI commands.

1.3 An Introduction to Touch Controllers

Capacitive sensing technology works by measuring the change in capacitance, which is the ability of a system to store an electric charge, within its field area, due to the presence of a conductive it could be any conductive object that has a different dielectric than air.

A common form of energy storage device is a parallel-plate capacitor. In a parallel plate capacitor, capacitance is directly proportional to the surface area of the conductor plates and inversely proportional to the separation distance between the plates

Capacitance is a function of the geometry of the design, the area of the plates and the distance between them and the permittivity of the dielectric material between the plates of the capacitor. For many dielectric materials, the permittivity and thus the capacitance, is independent of the potential difference between the conductors and the total charge on them.

A capacitor is thus essentially a sandwich of two pieces of conducting material separated by an insulating material, or dielectric.

1.4 Advantages of Capacitive Touch Sensor Technology

The main advantage of capacitive switches is that they do not have any moving parts or mechanical components, meaning there is less chance of failure. These types of devices are very clean looking with minimal crevices and openings, which reduces dirt and dust while also protecting against moisture. The flat surface also makes regular cleaning easier.

Early development of capacitive switches utilized printed circuit boards (PCBs), and the design possibilities have expanded by employing flexible printed circuits like flexible printed circuits (FPC) made from copper. This allows designers to utilize the technology in novel ways.

Some of the key advantages of capacitive touch technology are no moving mechanical components, improved reliability, back-lighting and haptic integration, easy wipe-down and cleaning, longevity and durability, design flexibility, modern aesthetics and integrating Capacitive Touch Sensor Technology.

There are many ways to integrate capacitive touch technology into a new product design. Often the simplest and most cost-effective approach is laminating a printed conductive layer to the underside of a touch surface. This can then be linked to a touch microcontroller.

This technology is not limited to flat surfaces. Thin, flexible circuits can conform to a variety of shapes and geometries, allowing touch-sensitive surfaces to fit in areas that would not be feasible with traditional switches. Touch-sensitive surfaces can be encapsulated in injection-moulded plastics, providing protection and simplifying final integration.

A primary goal in designing capacitive switches is to minimize external noises and enhance the signal strength for better performance. External interferences can potentially lead to false triggers and actuations or prevent the touch from being registered, which can affect the performance and function of the device.

Some of the key factors influencing design and performance include, external noise, feedback system, type of input, substrate materials, electro-magnetic interference (EMI) shielding, operating environment, product application, operating temperature, dielectric properties of overlay, electrical requirements, firmware, form-factor, gloved hands, internal noise, water and moisture.

An Introduction to MIDI

2.1 What is MIDI ?

MIDI is an acronym that stands for Musical Instrument Digital Interface. It is a technical standard digital communications protocol that allows computers, musical instruments and other hardware to connect audio devices together for playing, editing and recording music. MIDI also describes a digital interface, and electrical connectors for digital communication.

This allows one keyboard to trigger sounds on another synthesiser. Also virtual software synthesisers, which are computer programs that simulate hardware synthesisers, communicate with computer sequencing software running on the same computer using MIDI messages.

MIDI works as a digital signal. A series of binary digits (0s and 1s). Each instrument understands and then responds to these 1s and 0s, which are combined into 8-bit messages supporting data rates of up to 31,250 bits per second.

2.2 MIDI Channel and MIDI System Messages

MIDI messages consist of two main components:

1) MIDI Channel Messages,

2) MIDI System Messages.

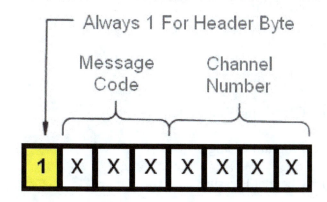

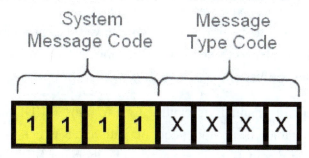

Figure 1: MIDI Channel and System Messages

The MIDI Channel Message Header Byte consists of a Message Code and a Channel Number. The Message Code 'xxx' can range from 000 to 110 in binary, which is 0 to 6 in decimal. So this allows for 7 different Channel Voice Message codes. The Channel Voice Messages are used to send musical performance information

The first half of the MIDI command byte (the three bits following the MSB) sets the type of command.

The 7 messages in this category are:

10000000 = Note Off,

10010000 = Note On,

10100000 = Aftertouch,

10110000 = Continuous Controller,

11000000 = Program Change,

11010000 = Channel Pressure,

11100000 = Pitch Bend.

The MIDI Channel Number 'xxxx' ranges in binary from 0000 to 1111, which is 0 to 15 in decimal. Note however that many MIDI systems often refer to these as MIDI Channels 1 to 16 (which can lead to some confusion).

The concept of channels is central to how most MIDI messages work. A channel is an independent path over which messages travel to their destination. There are 16 channels per MIDI device.

2.3 MIDI Note On Messages

In MIDI systems, the activation of a particular note and the release of the same note are considered as two separate events. When a key is pressed on a MIDI keyboard instrument or MIDI keyboard controller, the keyboard sends a Note On message on the MIDI OUT port.

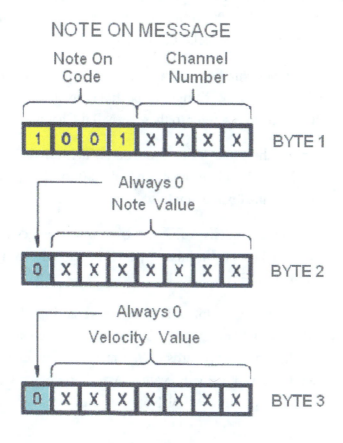

Figure 2: MIDI Note On Message

The keyboard may be set to transmit on any one of the sixteen logical MIDI channels, and the status byte for the Note On message will indicate the selected channel number. The Note On status byte is followed by two data bytes, which specify key number (indicating which key was pressed) and velocity (how hard the key was pressed). The key number is used in the receiving synthesiser to select which note should be played, and the velocity is normally used to control the amplitude of the note.

The Note On Message consists of three 8-bit bytes. Byte 1 contains the Note On command code and the MIDI Channel Number. The Note On code is 10010000 in binary, which is 144 in decimal and 0x90 in Hexadecimal, for MIDI Channel 1.

The MIDI Channel Number 'xxxx' ranges in binary from 0000 to 1111, which is 0 to 15 in decimal, respectively. Note however that most MIDI systems often refer to these as MIDI Channels 1 to 16.

Byte 2 contains the Note Value xxxxxxx which ranges in value from 0000000 to 1111111 in binary, which is 0 to 127 in decimal and 0x00 to 0x7F in Hexadecimal.

Byte 3 contains the Velocity Value xxxxxxx which ranges in value from 0000000 to 1111111 in binary, which is 0 to 127 in decimal and 0x00 to 0x7F in Hexadecimal.

Generally the harder you 'hit' a key on a keyboard the higher the velocity value, which produces a sound with a higher volume. Note though that some keyboards do not measure the velocity and instead output a fixed velocity value. Also a velocity value of 0000000 is equivalent to a MIDI Note Off message and switches the note off.

2.4 MIDI Note Off Messages

When the key is released, the keyboard instrument or controller will send a Note Off message. The Note Off message also includes data bytes for the key number and for the velocity with which the key was released.

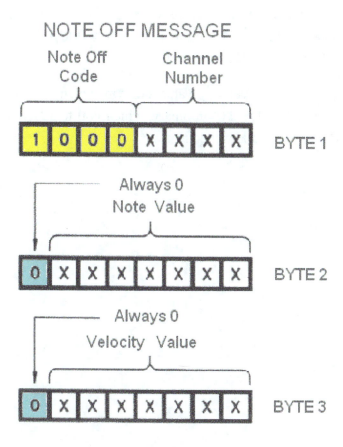

Figure 3: MIDI Note Off Message

The Note Off Message consists of three 8-bit bytes. Byte 1 contains the Note Off command code and the MIDI Channel Number. The Note Off code is 10000000 in binary, which is 128 in decimal and 0x80 in Hexadecimal, for MIDI Channel 1.

The MIDI Channel Number 'xxxx' ranges in binary from 0000 to 1111, which is 0 to 15 in decimal, respectively. Note however that most MIDI systems often refer to these as MIDI Channels 1 to 16.

Byte 2 contains the Note Value xxxxxxx which ranges in value from 0000000 to 1111111 in binary, which is 0 to 127 in decimal and 0x00 to 0x7F in Hexadecimal.

Byte 3 contains the Velocity Value xxxxxxx which ranges in value from 0000000 to 1111111 in binary, which is 0 to 127 in decimal and 0x00 to 0x7F in Hexadecimal.

2.5 MIDI Control Change Messages

MIDI Control Change messages are used to control a wide variety of functions in a synthesiser. Control Change messages, like other MIDI Channel messages, should only affect the Channel number indicated in the status byte. The Control Change status byte is followed by one data byte indicating the controller number, and a second byte which specifies the control value. The controller number identifies which function of the synthesiser is to be controlled by the message.

The MIDI Control Change Message consists of three 8-bit bytes. Byte 1 contains the MIDI Control Change command code and the MIDI Channel Number. The MIDI Control Change code is 10110000 in binary, which is 176 in decimal and 0xB0 in Hexadecimal, for MIDI Channel 1.

The MIDI Channel Number 'xxxx' ranges in binary from 0000 to 1111, which is 0 to 15 in decimal, respectively. Note however that most MIDI systems often refer to these as MIDI Channels 1 to 16.

Byte 2 contains the MIDI Control Change Number xxxxxxx which ranges in value from 0000000 to 1111111 in binary, which is 0 to 127 in decimal and 0x00 to 0x7F in Hexadecimal.

Byte 3 contains the MIDI Control Change Value xxxxxxx which ranges in value from 0000000 to 1111111 in binary, which is 0 to 127 in decimal and 0x00 to 0x7F in Hexadecimal.

MIDI keyboards often have Modulation and Pitch-Bend controller wheels. MIDI Modulation is a MIDI Control Change parameter with a MIDI Control Change Number equal to 1.

2.6 MIDI Pitch Bend

The Pitch Bend Change message is normally sent from a keyboard instrument in response to changes in position of the pitch bend wheel. The pitch bend information is used to modify the pitch of sounds being played on a given MIDI Channel.

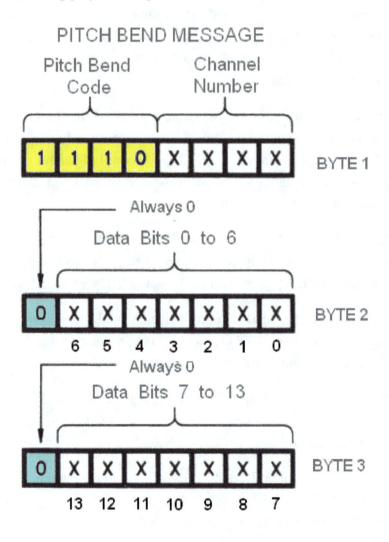

Figure 4: MIDI Pitch Bend Message

The Pitch Bend message includes two data bytes to specify the pitch bend value. Two bytes are required to allow fine enough resolution to make pitch changes resulting from movement of the pitch bend wheel seem to occur in a continuous manner rather than in steps.

The two bytes of the pitch bend message form a 14 bit number, 0 to 16383. The value 8192 (sent, LSB first, as 0x00 0x40), is centred, or "no pitch bend." The value 0 (0x00 0x00) means, "bend as low as possible," and, similarly, 16383 (0x7F 0x7F) is to "bend as high as possible." The exact range of the pitch bend is specific to the synthesiser.

2.7 MIDI Note Numbers for Different Octaves

Octave notation is given here in the International Organization for Standardization ISO system, ISO was formed to include/replace the American National Standards Institute (ANSI) and Deutsches Institut für Normung (DIN), the German standards institute.

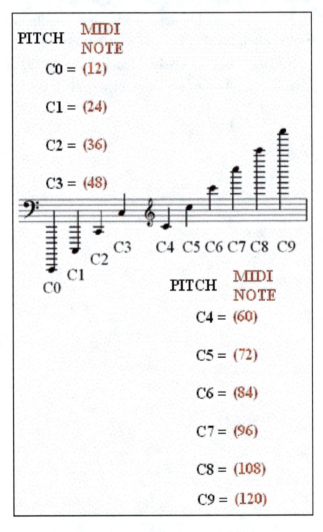

Figure 5: MIDI Note Numbers for Different Octaves

In this system, middle C (MIDI note number 60) is C4. A MIDI note number of 69 is used for A440 tuning, that is, the A note above middle C.

2.8 MIDI Note Numbers

The MIDI specification only defines note number 60 as "Middle C", and all other notes are relative. The absolute octave number designations shown here are based on Middle C = C4.

There is a discrepancy that occurs between various models of MIDI devices and software programs, and that concerns the octave numbers for note names. If your MIDI software/device considers octave 0 as being the lowest octave of the MIDI note range, then middle C's note name is C5. The lowest note name is then C0 (note number 0), and the highest possible note name is G10 (note number 127).

Some software/devices instead consider the third octave of the MIDI note range (2 octaves below middle C) as octave 0. In that case, the first 2 octaves are referred to as -2 and -1. So, middle C's note name is C3, the lowest note name is C-2, and the highest note name is G8.

A MIDI device can have up to 128 distinct pitches/notes, from 0 to 127 . But whereas musicians name the keys using the alphabetical names, with sharps and flats, and also octave numbers, this is more difficult for MIDI devices to process, so instead a unique number is assigned to each key.

Octave	Note Numbers											
	C	C#	D	D#	E	F	F#	G	G#	A	A#	B
-1	0	1	2	3	4	5	6	7	8	9	10	11
0	12	13	14	15	16	17	18	19	20	21	22	23
1	24	25	26	27	28	29	30	31	32	33	34	35
2	36	37	38	39	40	41	42	43	44	45	46	47
3	48	49	50	51	52	53	54	55	56	57	58	59
4	60	61	62	63	64	65	66	67	68	69	70	71
5	72	73	74	75	76	77	78	79	80	81	82	83
6	84	85	86	87	88	89	90	91	92	93	94	95
7	96	97	98	99	100	101	102	103	104	105	106	107
8	108	109	110	111	112	113	114	115	116	117	118	119
9	120	121	122	123	124	125	126	127				

Table 1: MIDI Note Numbers for different Octaves

The numbers used are 0 to 127. The lowest note upon a MIDI controller is a C and this is assigned note number 0. The C# above it would have a note number of 1. The D note above that would have a note number of 2. So "Middle C" is note number 60. A MIDI note number of 69 is used for A440 tuning, that is the A note above middle C.

MIDI Hardware

3.1 MIDI Hardware

A MIDI device is equipped with ports for MIDI IN, MIDI OUT and MIDI THRU. A special type of cable known as a MIDI cable is used to make these connections. Each wire is actually made of 3 wires, two are used for data transmission and one is a shield.

Each MIDI connection along one of these cables, can contain up to 16 channels of information and each MIDI device has 16 channels. Each one of these channels can have its own specified note, velocity, pitch bend etc.

It gets slightly confusing as MIDI signals can now be transferred via USB. This is common in most modern synthesisers or MIDI keyboards. The USB effectively takes the place of the In, Out and Thru ports.

3.2 The MIDI IN Port

The MIDI IN schematic circuit diagram consists of a 5-pin DIN 180 degree socket connected to, IC1, a 6N139 high speed opto-isolator, via, R1, a 220 ohm resistor. The input is wired in current loop mode which helps avoid earth loop problems. The IN4148 diode, D1, prevents reverse current problems to the opto-isolator, if an external MIDI cable is connected incorrectly.

The output of the opto-isolator is connected to the RX pin of the Arduino. The opto-isolator is also connected to the 5V (Volt) and GND (Ground) pins of the Arduino.

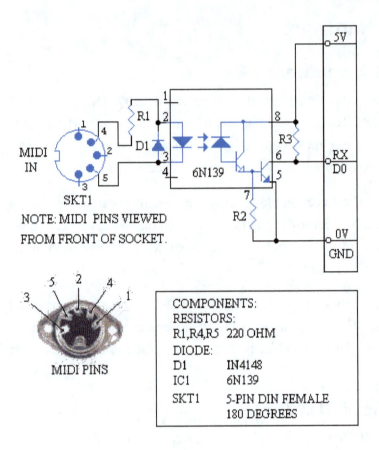

Figure 6: MIDI IN Schematic Drawing

3.3 MIDI IN and MIDI THRU Ports

The MIDI THRU schematic consists of the addition of two Schmitt-trigger Inverters to the MIDI IN circuit. The MIDI THRU design uses the SN74LS14N which is a Hex Schmitt-trigger Inverter, temperature compensated and can be triggered from the slowest of input ramps and still give clean, jitter-free output signals. Each circuit functions as an inverter, but because of the Schmitt action, it has different input threshold levels for positive-going (VT+) and negative-going (VT-) signals.

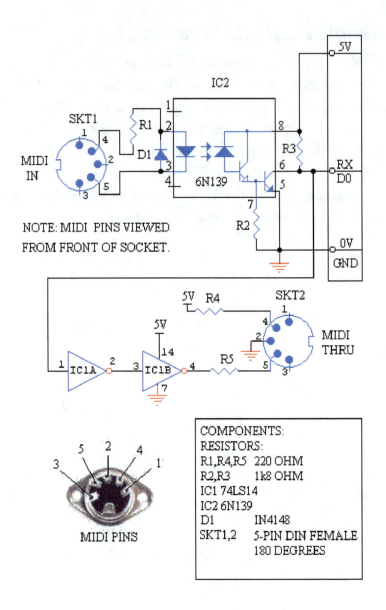

Figure 7: MIDI IN and THRU Schematic Drawing

3.4 MIDI OUT Port wiring

The MIDI OUT schematic circuit diagram consists of a 5-pin DIN 180 degree socket connected to two 220 ohm resistors. One of the 220 ohm resistors is connected to the +5 Volt (5V) pin of the Arduino and the other 220 ohm resistor is connected to the TX pin.

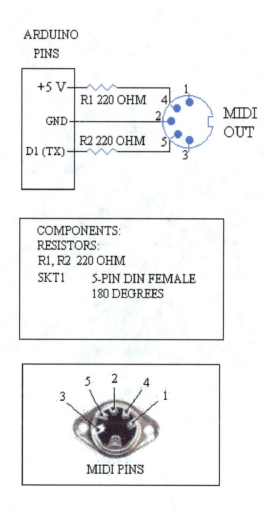

Figure 8: MIDI OUT Schematic Drawing

Pin 2 of the DIN socket is connected to the GND (GROUND) pin of the Arduino. This ground connection is usually connected to the screen of the MIDI cable which is connected to the MIDI socket. This is useful to prevent electrical interference being picked up from stray electrical fields along the cable length. The MIDI cable maximum length is specified as 15 metres.

Figure 9: MIDI OUT Wiring Diagram

3.5 The Arduino MIDI IN/OUT Board

The Arduino MIDI IN/OUT board is designed so that it can be plugged into the Arduino Uno or Arduino Mega 2560 board directly and connect to digital pins D0 to D7, while still allowing access to all the other pins.

Figure 10: The Arduino MIDI IN/OUT Board

Pins D0 and D1 are connected to the RX and TX pins, respectively. Arduino Pins D2 and D3 require +5 Volt and 0 Volt(GND), respectively, and these voltages are provided in the software with these lines:

```
pinMode(2, OUTPUT);
```

```
  pinMode(3, OUTPUT);
// GND 0 Volt supply to opto-coupler
  digitalWrite(3, LOW);
 // +5 Volt supply to opto-coupler
  digitalWrite(2, HIGH);
```

Then you need to set Arduino Pins D4, D5, D6 and D7, as digital input pins with internal pull-up resistors. These are connected to the 4-way DIL switch, to select the MIDI Channel (1 to 16), with these lines:

```
// Set Inputs for 4 way DIP Switch
  pinMode(4, INPUT_PULLUP);
  pinMode(5, INPUT_PULLUP);
  pinMode(6, INPUT_PULLUP);
  pinMode(7, INPUT_PULLUP);
```

The 4-way DIP switches are read, shifted and added to produce a sum between 0 and 15 for the MIDI Channel. However the Arduino MIDI Library software requires MIDI Channel values between 1 to 16. So 1 is added to the 'MIDIchannel' variable, as shown in this section of code:

```
// Read 4-way DIP switch
  MIDIchannel = digitalRead(4) + (digitalRead(5)
<< 1) + (digitalRead(6) << 2) + (digitalRead(7)
<< 3);
  MIDIchannel = MIDIchannel + 1;
```

The lines:

```
#include <MIDI.h>
MIDI_CREATE_DEFAULT_INSTANCE();
```

call the MIDI Library functions and initialises MIDI with:

```
  MIDI.begin(MIDI_CHANNEL_OMNI);
```

The MIDI Channel is selected by the 4-way DIP switches.

DIP Switch Selections				MIDI Channel
4	3	2	1	
on	on	on	on	1
on	on	on	off	2
on	on	off	on	3
on	on	off	off	4
on	off	on	on	5
on	off	on	off	6
on	off	off	on	7
on	off	off	off	8
off	on	on	on	9
off	on	on	off	10
off	on	off	on	11
off	on	off	off	12
off	off	on	on	13
off	off	on	off	14
off	off	off	on	15
off	off	off	off	16
MIDI Channel Selection				

Table 2: DIP switch MIDI channel (1-16) setting

The 4-way DIP switches are a set of electrical switches packaged in a small box or housing. They are designed to be mounted on printed circuit boards to provide a range of electrical inputs to an electronic device based on the position of the individual switches. Each of the 4 switches can be set to the On or Off position. With the 4 switches you have 16 different selections, as shown in Table 2. The switches can be used for the selection of a MIDI Channel from 1 to 16.

MIDI TOUCH MUSICAL INSTRUMENTS USING THE ARDUINO

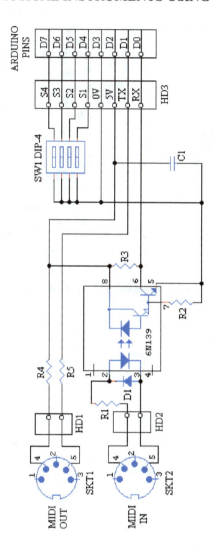

Figure 11: MIDI IN and OUT Board Circuit Schematic Drawing

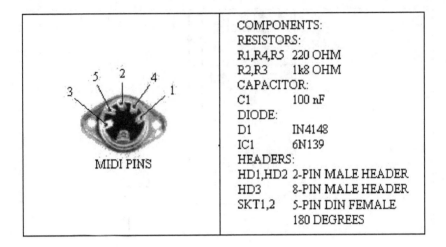

COMPONENTS:
RESISTORS:
R1,R4,R5 220 OHM
R2,R3   1k8 OHM
CAPACITOR:
C1   100 nF
DIODE:
D1   IN4148
IC1   6N139
HEADERS:
HD1,HD2 2-PIN MALE HEADER
HD3   8-PIN MALE HEADER
SKT1,2   5-PIN DIN FEMALE
               180 DEGREES

MIDI PINS

Figure 12: Components for the MIDI IN and OUT Board Circuit

3.6 Arduino MIDI IN/OUT Library Installation

The MIDI IN/OUT board requires the software from the Arduino MIDI Library, which is available at:

https://www.arduino.cc/reference/en/libraries/midi-library/

This library is compatible with all architectures so you should be able to use it on all the Arduino boards. To use this library, open the Library Manager in the Arduino IDE and install it from there:

https://www.arduino.cc/en/Guide/Libraries

3.7 MIDI/USB Installation by Updating the Atmega16U2 using Device Firmware Update (DFU)

The ATmega16U2 chip on the Arduino Uno or Mega 2560 board acts as a bridge between the computer's USB port and the main processor's serial port. The chip is used for USB serial communications and allows the boards to be programmed via the Arduino IDE. The ATmega16U2 chip runs firmware that can be updated through a special USB protocol called Device Firmware Update (DFU).

The firmware on the ATmega16U2 can be updated in a few steps.

1) Connect the Arduino to your computer via a USB cable

2) Reset the ATmega16U2.

To do this, briefly bridge the reset pin 5 with the ground pin 6. The pins are located near the USB connector, connect them briefly with a piece of wire.

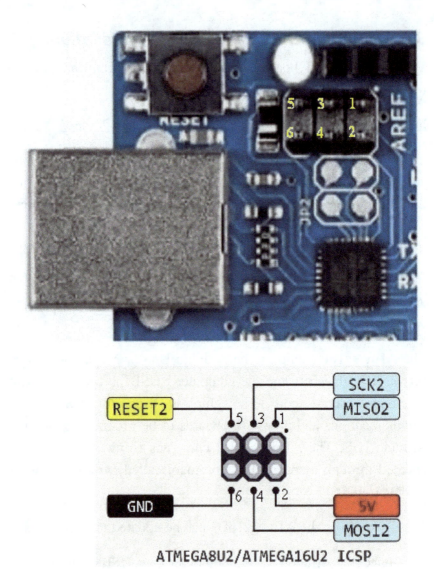

Figure 13: Pin Connections for ATmega16u2 ICSP

To verify you have reset the Atmega16u2 chip look in the Arduino programming environment, and check the list of serial ports. The serial port for the board should no longer show up.

3.8 Download the Flexible In-system Programmer (FLIP)

To perform a firmware upgrade, Atmel has developed a Flexible in-system programmer (FLIP). This software allows performing in-System Programming from a USB host controller without removing the part from the system or without a preprogrammed application, and without any external programming interface.

The FLIP program can be downloaded from:

https://www.microchip.com/en-us/development-tool/flip

3.9 The Dual Moco LUFA Project

This is dual mode firmware for the Mega16U2 chip on the Arduino Uno or Mega. There are two modes on this firmware, USB-MIDI(MocoLUFA) and Arduino-Serial. So this allows the Arduino Uno and Mega to operate in standard MIDI mode via the USB connection. It defaults to standard MIDI Baud rate of 31250. By replacing the original firmware on Mega16U2, the Arduino will act as USB-MIDI device (Standard Midi Class). You do not need to install additional device drivers on Windows, MaxOSX, and Linux, as the firmware acts as a device of Standard Midi Class. It will automatically install on the system as an Audio USB Device.

The dualMocoLUFA Project was developed by Morecat Lab and the details are at:

http://morecatlab.akiba.coocan.jp/lab/index.php/aruino/midi-firmware-for-arduino-uno-moco/?lang=en

You can download the dualMoco.hex file at:

https://github.com/kuwatay/mocolufa/tree/master/HEX

Further details for updating the Atmega8U2 and 16U2 on an Uno or Mega2560 using DFU:

https://www.arduino.cc/en/Hacking/DFUProgramming8U2

Note that the dualMocoLUFA works on the ATmega16U2 chip (but not on the ATmega8U2 chip, which was used on earlier versions of the Uno).

3.10 Uploading the hex file dualMOCO.hex to the Arduino board using FLIP

Use the programme FLIP to upload the hex file dualMOCO.hex to the Arduino board.

Select Atmega16u2 in Devices

1. Connect the target hardware to the host platform via USB.

2. Select a device from the device list.

From the top menu bar, select the Device item. In the Device pull-down menu, click the Select item. Select Atmega16u2 in Devices.

3. Select a communication medium.

From the top menu bar, select the Settings item. In the Settings pull-down menu, click the Communication item. In the Communication cascading menu, select the USB communication medium.

The medium setup dialog box pops up. Adjust the communication parameters, and click Connect.

4. Select a HEX data file.

From the top menu bar, select the File item. In the File pull-down menu, click the Load HEX File item. Select the dualMoco.hex HEX file from the file browser.

5) Select Run to program the dualMoco.hex file into the ATmega16u2

The dual MOCO/MIDI firmware is installed and will be recognised as a USB Audio Driver and and operate as a device of Standard Midi Class.

3.11 Programming the Uno or Mega2560 containing MIDI MOCO/LUFA Firmware

The steps to program the UNO or MEGA board are:

1) Remove all USB (and power) connections from the board.

2) Connect a jumper between pin 4 and pin 6 on ICSP for USB interface connector for Mega16U2.

3) Connect a USB connection to the board, from the computer.

4) Wait for USB driver to be automatically installed.

5) Arduino Serial mode is initiated.

6) Use Arduino IDE to program Mega2560 (or Uno) board.

Once your board is programmed you can return to MIDI MOCO/LUFA mode by :

1) Unplugging your board from the USB connector.

2) Removing the jumper from between pin 4 and pin 6 on ICSP for USB interface.

3) Re-connecting the USB connector.

4) The board is now in MIDI MOCO/LUFA mode and will be recognised as as a USB Audio Driver, and operates as a device of Standard Midi Class.

An Introduction to the Arduino

4.1 What is the Arduino?

The Arduino is an open-source electronics platform based on easy-to-use hardware and software. Arduino designs and manufactures single-board microcontrollers and microcontroller kits for building digital devices. The Arduino single-board microcontroller boards are able to read inputs, make decisions and produce outputs. The Arduino board can be programmed by sending a set of instructions to the microcontroller on the board. To do so you use the Arduino programming language (based on Wiring), and the Arduino Software IDE (Integrated Development Environment), based on Processing.

4.2 Arduino Board Types

There are a large number of Arduino boards available. The 2 board types used for these MIDI design projects are the Arduino UNO and the Arduino MEGA 2560.

Arduino board designs use a variety of microprocessors and microcontrollers. The boards are equipped with sets of digital and analogue input/output (I/O) pins that may be interfaced to various expansion boards and other circuits. The boards feature serial communications interfaces, including Universal Serial Bus (USB) on some models, which are also used for loading programs.

4.3 Arduino Board Description

Some boards have different features from those given below, but most Arduinos have the majority of these components in common:

Reset Button – This will restart any code that is loaded to the Arduino board,

AREF – Stands for "Analog Reference" and is used to set an external reference voltage,

Ground Pin – There are a few ground pins on the Arduino,

Digital Input/Output – Pins 0-13 can be used for digital input or output,

PWM – The pins marked with the (~) symbol can simulate analog output,

USB Connection – Used for powering up the Arduino and uploading sketches,

ATmega Microcontroller – This is the brains and is where the programs are stored,

Crystal Oscillator – The crystal oscillator sets the basic time of operation of the Arduino. The number printed on top of the Arduino crystal is 16.000Hz, which is a frequency of 16,000,000 Hertz or 16 MHz,

Power LED Indicator – This LED lights up anytime the board is plugged in a power source,

DC Power Barrel Jack – This is used for powering your Arduino with a power supply,

Voltage Regulator – The function of the voltage regulator is to control the voltage sent to the Arduino board and stabilize the DC voltages used by the processor and other elements,

3.3V Pin – This pin supplies 3.3 volts of power to your projects,

5V Pin – This pin supplies 5 volts of power to your projects,

Analog Pins – These pins can read the signal from an analog sensor and convert it to digital data.

ICSP pins – The ICSP is a tiny programming header for the Arduino consisting of MOSI, MISO, SCK, RESET, VCC, and GND. It is often referred to as an SPI (Serial Peripheral Interface), which could be considered as an "expansion" of the output,

TX and RX LEDs – On the board, there are two labels: TX (transmit) and RX (receive). They appear in two places on the Arduino UNO board. First, at the digital pins 0 and 1, to indicate the pins responsible for serial communication. Second, the TX and RX led. The TX led flashes with different speed while sending the serial data. The speed of flashing depends on the baud rate used by the board. RX flashes during the receiving process.

The Arduino Uno needs a power source in order for it to operate and can be powered in a variety of ways. You can connect the board directly to your computer via a USB cable. If you want your project to be mobile, you can use a 9V battery pack to give it power. The last method would be to use a 9V DC power supply.

4.4 Arduino Installation

First you must have an Arduino board and a USB cable. In case you use Arduino UNO, Arduino Duemilanove, Nano, Arduino Mega 2560, or Diecimila, you will need a standard USB cable (A plug to B plug), the kind you would connect to a USB printer.

You can get different versions of the Arduino IDE from the Download page on the Arduino Official website, at:

https://www.arduino.cc/en/software

You then select the software, which is compatible with your operating system (Windows, IOS, or Linux). After your file download is complete, unzip the file.

The Arduino Software (IDE) allows you to write programs and upload them to your board. In the Arduino Software page you will find two options:

If you have a reliable Internet connection, you could use the online IDE (Arduino Web Editor). It will allow you to save your sketches in the cloud, having them available from any device and backed up. You will always have the most up-to-date version of the IDE without the need to install updates or community generated libraries. If you would rather work offline, you should use the latest version of the desktop IDE.

Then you power up the board. The Arduino Uno, Mega, Duemilanove and Arduino Nano automatically draw power from either, the USB connection to the computer or an external power supply.

After your Arduino IDE software is downloaded, you need to unzip the folder. Inside the folder, you can find the application icon with an infinity label (application.exe). Double-click the icon to start the IDE.

Now launch the Arduino IDE. Once the software starts, you can Create a new project or Open an existing project example. To create a new project, select File → New. To open an existing project example, select File → Example → Basics → Blink.

This is just one of the program examples called "Blink". It turns the LED on and off with some time delay. You can select any other example from the list.

Then you select your Arduino board. To avoid any error while uploading your program to the board, you must select the correct Arduino board name, which matches with the board connected to your computer.

Go to the Menu → Tools → Board and select your board. Then you select the name matching the board that you are using.

Next select the serial device of the Arduino board. Go to Tools → Serial Port menu. This is likely to be COM3 or higher (COM1 and COM2 are usually reserved for hardware serial ports). To find out, you can disconnect your Arduino board and re-open the menu, the entry that disappears should be of the Arduino board. Reconnect the board and select that serial port.

Now, simply click the "Upload" button in the environment. Wait a few seconds; you will see the RX and TX LEDs on the board, flashing. If the upload is successful, the message "Done uploading" will appear in the status bar.

Note: If you are Uploading an Arduino program you need to make sure that the MIDI IN cable is not connected, as MIDI IN uses the same serial pin (RX) on the Arduino, and will prevent the program data from uploading. If you leave the MIDI OUT connected the program will upload fine, but be aware that you will be sending random MIDI data to the external MIDI device, which can cause problems. For example it may change the sounds in a synthesiser memory bank.

Listing 1: Simplest Arduino Sketch

This code contains two functions:

The first one is setup(). Anything you put in this function will be executed by the Arduino just once when the program starts.

The second one is loop(). Once the Arduino finishes with the code in the setup() function, it will move into a loop(), and it will continue running it in a loop, again and again, until you reset it or cut off the power.

Notice that both setup() and loop() have open and close parenthesis. Functions can receive parameters, which is a way by which the program can pass data between its different functions. The setup and loop functions don't have any parameters passed to them. Every single sketch you write will have these two functions in it, even if you don't use them.

4.5 The Arduino UNO Rev 3

The Arduino Uno is a microcontroller board based on the ATmega328P. It has 14 digital input/output pins (of which 6 can be used as PWM outputs), 6 analog inputs, a 16 MHz ceramic resonator, a USB connection, a power jack, an ICSP header and a reset button. It contains everything needed to support the microcontroller; simply connect it to a computer with a USB cable or power it with a AC-to-DC adapter or battery to get started.

Full information on the Arduino UNO Rev 3 is available at:

https://docs.arduino.cc/hardware/uno-rev3

Microcontroller	ATmega328P
Operating Voltage	5V
Input Voltage (recommended)	7-12V
Input Voltage (limit)	6-20V
Digital I/O Pins	14 (of which 6 provide PWM output)
PWM Digital I/O Pins	6
Analog Input Pins	6
DC Current per I/O Pin	20 mA
DC Current for 3.3V Pin	50 mA
Flash Memory	32 KB (ATmega328P) of which 0.5 KB used by bootloader
SRAM	2 KB (ATmega328P)
EEPROM	1 KB (ATmega328P)
Clock Speed	16 MHz
LED_BUILTIN	13
Length	68.6 mm
Width	53.4 mm
Weight	25 g

Table 3: The Arduino UNO Specifications

4.6 The Arduino MEGA 2560

The Arduino Mega 2560 is a microcontroller board based on the ATmega2560. It has 54 digital input/output pins (of which 15 can be used as PWM outputs), 16 analog inputs, 4 UARTs (hardware serial ports), a 16 MHz crystal oscillator, a USB connection, a power jack, an ICSP header, and a reset button.

Full information on the Arduino Mega 2560 is available at:

https://www.arduino.cc/en/Guide/ArduinoMega2560

Microcontroller	ATmega2560
Operating Voltage	5V
Input Voltage (recommended)	7-12V
Input Voltage (limit)	6-20V
Digital I/O Pins	54 (15 provide PWM output)
Analog Input Pins	16
DC Current per I/O Pin	20 mA
DC Current for 3.3V Pin	50 mA
Flash Memory	256 KB, with 8 K bootloader
SRAM	8 KB
EEPROM	4 KB
Clock Speed	16 MHz
LED_BUILTIN	13
Length	101.52 mm
Width	53.3 mm
Weight	37 g

Table 4: Arduino Mega 2560 Specifications

Arduino Testing

5.1 Arduino Software and Hardware Testing

For projects that combine software and hardware it is good practice to be able to have simple programs to enable the testing of both elements. One simple example is to use the Arduino microcontroller board with a program to switch the internal LED (Light Emitting Diode) On and Off. This tests that the program has been uploaded correctly and that the LED hardware is also working.

5.2 Arduino LED Test Blink program

The main functions of the 'Blink' program are:

- Turn on the LED

- Wait for one second

- Turn off the LED

- Wait for one second

- Repeat turning LED on and off.

```
//  Blinking LED
// Turns on an LED on for one second, then off for
one second,
// repeatedly.

const int LED = 13;
// the setup function runs once when you press reset
or power on // the board
void setup() {
// initialize digital pin 13 as an output.
```

```
  pinMode(LED, OUTPUT);
}

// the loop function runs over and over again
forever
void loop() {
// turn the LED on (HIGH is the voltage level)
  digitalWrite(LED, HIGH);
  delay(1000);                    // wait for a second
// turn the LED off by making the voltage LOW
  digitalWrite(LED, LOW);
  delay(1000);                    // wait for a second
}
```

Listing 2: Blink Program for On-board LED

MIDI Software and Hardware

6.1 MIDI Software and Hardware Requirements

There are a number of items which may be needed for testing the MIDI Software and Hardware, such as:

An Arduino board, a cable type male USB A to male USB B, for programming or powering the Arduino board. A MIDI/USB cable or a MIDI/USB interface unit, to connect the MIDI OUT to a computer. Some designs require the MIDI IN, MIDI OUT or MIDI THRU hardware ports. A MIDI hardware or software synthesiser or MIDI module.

Figure 14: Arduino and male USB A to male USB B cable

Figure 15: A MIDI/USB Interface Cable

The Arduino UNO and Mega 2560 boards can be powered from the USB socket or via the external power connector. External power can come either from an AC-to-DC adapter or battery. The adapter can be connected by plugging a centre-positive plug with an internal diameter of 2.1mm, an external diameter of 5.5mm and 12mm long, into the board's power jack. Leads from a battery can be inserted in the Gnd and Vin pin headers of the POWER connector. A low dropout regulator provides improved energy efficiency.

The board can operate on an external supply of 7 to 20 volts. If supplied with less than 7V, however, the 5V pin may supply less than five volts and the board may be unstable. If using more than 12V, the voltage regulator may overheat and damage the board. The recommended range is 7 to 12 volts, capable of supplying about 1 Amp, which is 12 Watt (W) with a 12 Volt supply.. Note that the power input selection is automatically selected.

6.2 MIDI Monitoring

Note that MIDI operates at a BAUD rate of 31250, which is not one of the available choices in the Arduino Serial Monitor screen. So MIDI needs to be monitored with a special MIDI program.

Pocket MIDI is a MIDI monitoring tool for Windows and Mac. Connect your MIDI instrument to computer using a USB or USB/MIDI adapter and you can monitor MIDI messages to and from your instrument in real time. You can also send message from the application to your instrument. Pocket MIDI(for Windows/Mac) is freeware.

https://www.morson.jp/pocketmidi-webpage/

MidiView is a simple MIDI Monitor app, for Windows and Mac, that shows bi-directional MIDI packages that flow through your computer.

https://hautetechnique.com/midi/midiview/

MIDI-OX is a Windows 32 bit program., the world's greatest all-purpose MIDI Utility!

http://www.midiox.com/

Midi Monitoris a powerful tool to learn about Midi, to setup a Midi configuration and to exchange Midi System exclusive data. Midi channel messages real time monitoring.

http://obds.free.fr/midimon/

MIDI Monitor (Mac only) is an app to display MIDI signals going in and out of your Mac. Musicians will find it handy for tracking down confusing MIDI problems, and programmers can use it to test MIDI drivers and applications. MIDI Monitor is free to download and use.

https://www.snoize.com/midimonitor/

6.3 MIDI IN to OUT Activity Detector LED

This program lights the onboard LED whenever it detects MIDI IN activity on the RX pin. It also sends transfers the MIDI Input data to the Output TX Pin. So this tests the input and output pins for correct MIDI transmission.

```
// MIDI IN Activity Detector
// Program requires the MIDI IN and OUT
hardware

 #define LedPin 13

byte midiByte;

void setup() {
  pinMode(LedPin, OUTPUT);
  digitalWrite(LedPin, LOW);
  Serial.begin(31250); // set MIDI baud rate
  Serial.flush();
}

void loop() {
  if (Serial.available() > 0) {
    digitalWrite(LedPin, HIGH);
    // read the incoming byte:
    midiByte = Serial.read();
    // send the byte to the output
    Serial.write(midiByte);
    delay(1);
    digitalWrite(LedPin, LOW);
  }
}
```

Listing 3: MIDI IN Activity Detector

Note: When uploading the MIDI Activity Detector program make sure to disconnect the MIDI IN socket, because it uses the same RX Arduino Pin which is used for programming the Arduino. If the MIDI IN connection is not removed, then trying to program the Arduino will fail.

6.4 Explanation of the source code

The program consists of three parts. The first part is where we 'declare' our constants and variables, the second part is the section of code called void setup(), and the third is the void loop().

All code between the curly brackets after the void setup() will be executed once, at the start of the program. All code between the curly brackets after void loop() will be executed repeatedly (after void setup() has run) until the program is powered off.

The statements:

```
pinMode(LedPin, OUTPUT);
digitalWrite(LedPin, LOW);
```

make the LedPin an Output and turns the LedPin LOW, which means the LED will be Off.

The statements:

```
Serial.begin(31250); // set MIDI baud rate
Serial.flush();
```

sets the Serial Output to the MIDI Baud rate of 31250 and then clears the Serial output.

The statement:

```
if (Serial.available() > 0) {
```

tests to see if any incoming MIDI data is available. If MIDI data is available the data is read using

```
midiByte = Serial.read();
```

and then the variable 'midiByte' is written to the TX port, using:

```
Serial.write(midiByte);
```

Design Considerations for Capacitive Touch Projects

Circuits that have both resistive and capacitive elements take time to charge and discharge. During that time, the voltage across the capacitor is constantly changing.

7.1 Charging a Capacitor

The voltage across the capacitor (Vc) is dependent on the source voltage Vs, and the exponential value of the ratio of the time(t) to the resistance (R) and Capacitance (C):

$$Vc = Vs(1 - e^{(-t/RC)})$$

So for example, when t = RC then the capacitor voltage Vc is:

$$Vc = Vs(1 - 2.718^{(-1)}) = Vs(1 - 0.37) = 0.63 \times Vs$$

So the capacitor reaches 63% of the final value in the first Time Constant (RC) when charging.

Charging Capacitor

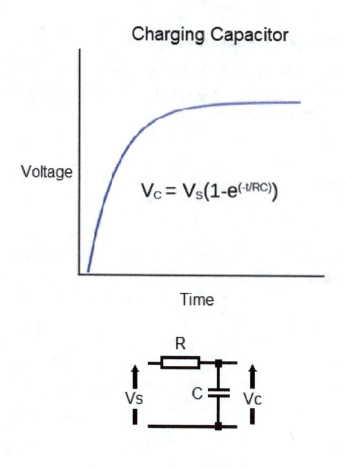

Voltage

$$V_C = V_S(1-e^{(-t/RC)})$$

Time

R

Vs   C   Vc

Vc = Capacitor Voltage
Vs = Source Voltage
e = Exponential e (approx. 2.718)
t = Time in Seconds
R = Resistance in Ohms
C = Capacitance in Farads

Figure 16: Diagram and Equation for Charging Capacitor

7.2 Discharging a Capacitor

The voltage across the capacitor (Vc) is dependent on the source voltage Vs, and the exponential value of the ratio of the time(t) to the resistance (R) and Capacitance (C):

$$Vc = Vs(e^{-t/RC})$$

So for example, when t = RC then the capacitor voltage Vc is:

$$Vc = Vs(2.718^{(-1)}) = Vs(0.37) = 0.37 \times Vs$$

So the capacitor reaches 37% of the final value in the first Time Constant (RC) when discharging.

Discharging Capacitor

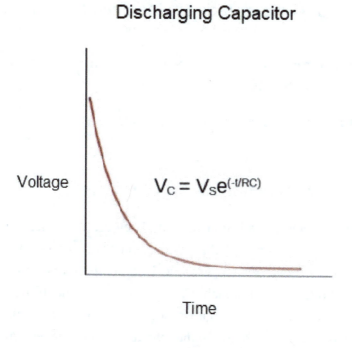

Voltage

$$V_C = V_S e^{(-t/RC)}$$

Time

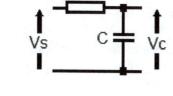

Vc = Capacitor Voltage
Vs = Source Voltage
e = Exponential e (approx. 2.718)
t = Time in Seconds
R = Resistance in Ohms
C = Capacitance in Farads

Figure 17: Diagram and Equation for Discharging Capacitor

7.3 *Arduino Considerations for Touch Control for MIDI*

There are a number of elements to consider for all the Arduino boards for touch control for MIDI:

- The Threshold On Voltage/Time,

- The Threshold Off Voltage/Time,

- The Latency for MIDI switching.

These three elements are all inter-related. They are dependent on the RC combination for the charge and discharge times. The operating source voltage for the Arduino Uno and Mega boards is fixed at +5 Volts. Human touch Capacitance is about 100 pF (PicoFarads). So the main design choice in the projects is the choice of resistance (R). The resistance value can vary depending on the proximity of operation requirement. But also it can effect the MIDI switching time latency.

So for example, if the resistance was 1M ohm and the capacitance was 100 pF then the RC Time Constant would be:

$RC = 1x\ 10^6\ x\ 100\ x10^{-12}\ x\ 10^6$ uS (micro-seconds)

which is 100 uS. This would allow the capacitor voltage value to reach 63% of the final value in 100 uS. So generally this is fast enough to allow polyphonic MIDI transmissions.

Most of the MIDI Touch Control projects in the book allow the initial setting of the On and Off Thresholds.

7.4 Grounding and other known issues

The grounding of the Arduino microcontroller board is *very* important in capacitive sensing. The board needs to have some connection to an earth ground, like a low-impedance path such as a wire attached to a metal water pipe. Connecting the charging cord to the laptop will usually be enough to get things working correctly.

Capacitive sensing has some quirks with laptops which are not connected to mains power. The laptop itself tends to become sensitive and bringing a hand near the laptop will change the returned values.

Another solution that seems to have worked well on some installations, is to run a foil ground plane under the sensor foil (insulated by plastic, paper, etc.), and connected by a wire to ground.

7.5 Software Considerations

Note that the MIDI Touch designs require touch input resistors for all the inputs that are scanned. If a touch input resistor is not included for a scanned input then the design can get stuck in an infinite loop and will not work correctly.

Capacitive Touch Sensor to Serial Out

This design uses the Arduino UNO and the Serial Output. Connect a wire to pin 8 of the Arduino. Then connect the end of the wire to the 1M ohm resistor, which is in turn connected to pin 10.

Figure 18: Wiring Layout for Touch Sensor Capacitive Input

The Arduino periodically sends out pulses and measures how much time elapses until it receives a response. When the user comes closer to the piece of metal that forms the first plate of the sensor, the Arduino can detect a change in the timing and use that information to determine whether the user made a touch input.

8.1 Source Code for Capacitive Touch Sensor to Serial Out

```
#define SensorOut 10
#define SensorIn 8

void setup() {
  pinMode(SensorOut, OUTPUT);
  pinMode(SensorIn, INPUT);
  Serial.begin(9600);
}

void loop() {
  digitalWrite(SensorOut, LOW);
  delay(10);
  long startTime = micros();
  digitalWrite(SensorOut, HIGH);
  while (digitalRead(SensorIn) == LOW);
  long sensorVal = micros() - startTime;
  Serial.println (sensorVal);
}
```

Listing 4: Source Code for Capacitive Sensor to Serial Out

8.2 Explanation of the Source Code

Start by defining two pins as input and output of the sensor:

```
#define SensorOut 10
#define SensorIn 8
```

Use pinMode() to set the sensor pins as Output and Input, and set the Serial Output to work at 9600 Baud:

```
pinMode(SensorOut, OUTPUT);
pinMode(SensorIn, INPUT);
Serial.begin(9600);
```

Now that the initialization is complete, it is time to get to the main part, the loop. First, set SensorOut to LOW and then delay by 10 milliseconds. This makes sure that there is no noise in the sensor before you take the reading and also limits the speed at which the data will be printed on the Serial monitor. Then create a long integer variable called startTime and set it to micros().

```
void loop() {
  digitalWrite(SensorOut, LOW);
  delay(10);
  long startTime = micros();
```

Now, set SensorOut to HIGH and start a WHILE loop which should run until SensorIn no longer detects a low signal. After the while loop has stopped, create another variable called sensorVal and set it to the difference between micros() and start time. Finally, print it on the Serial monitor.

```
digitalWrite(SensorOut, HIGH);
while (digitalRead(SensorIn) == LOW);
```

```
long sensorVal = micros() - startTime;
Serial.println (sensorVal);
```

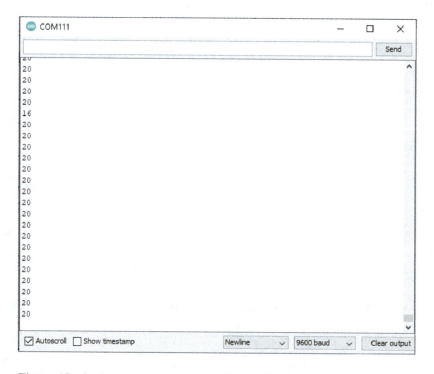

Figure 19 : Serial Out for untouched Capacitive Input

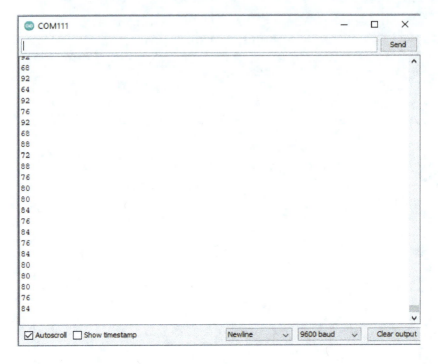

Figure 20: Serial Out for Touched Capacitive Input

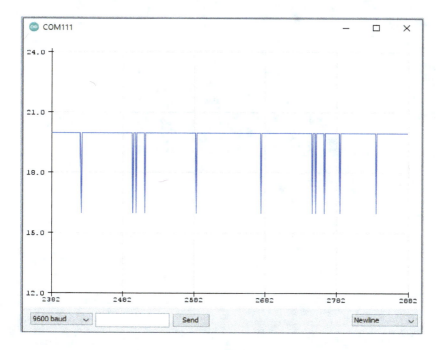

Figure 21: Serial Plotter Out for Untouched Capacitive Input

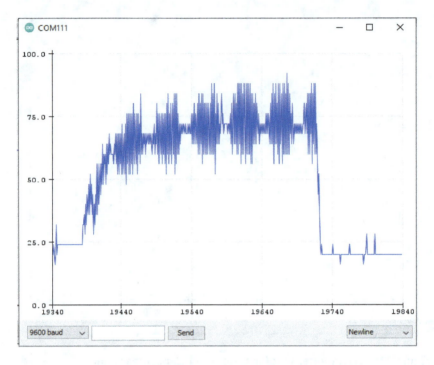

Figure 22: Serial Plotter Out for Touched Capacitive Input

The serial Plotter Out for the Touched Capacitive Input shows the value increasing from about 25 to over 75 as the finger moves towards the touch input. Then when the finger is removed the value returns to less than 25.

A Capacitive Touch Sensor to Built-in LED Out

This program detects the capacitive touch value and if it is greater than the pre-programmed threshold value then the Built-In LED is turned ON, otherwise it is turned OFF.

Figure 23: Capacitive Touch Sensor to Built-In LED

9.1 Source Code for Capacitive Touch Sensor to Built-In LED

```
#define SensorOut 10
#define SensorIn 8
const int touchVal = 31;
```

```
void setup() {
  pinMode(SensorOut, OUTPUT);
  pinMode(SensorIn, INPUT);
  pinMode(LED_BUILTIN, OUTPUT);
  Serial.begin(9600);
}

void loop() {
  digitalWrite(SensorOut, LOW);
  delay(10);
  long startTime = micros();
  digitalWrite(SensorOut, HIGH);
  while (digitalRead(SensorIn) == LOW);
  long sensorVal = micros() - startTime;
  Serial.println (sensorVal);
  if (sensorVal > touchVal)
digitalWrite(LED_BUILTIN, HIGH);
  else digitalWrite(LED_BUILTIN, LOW);
}
```

Listing 5: Capacitive Sensor to Serial and LED Out

9.2 Explanation of the Source Code

This program is similar to the previous program. But has the addition of lighting the in-built LED when the sensor is touched. The in-built LED is set as an Output:

```
pinMode(LED_BUILTIN, OUTPUT);
```

The in-built LED is switched ON or OFF using the IF/ELSE function:

```
if (sensorVal > touchVal)
digitalWrite(LED_BUILTIN, HIGH);
  else digitalWrite(LED_BUILTIN, LOW);
```

Capacitive Sensor to LED Output using a Pulse Width Modulation (PWM) Output Pin

This circuit detects how close you are to touching the Touch Input pin and generates a Pulse Width Modulation (PWM) signal which is connected to an external LED via a 220 ohm resistor. The closer you are to the Touch Input the brighter the LED gets.

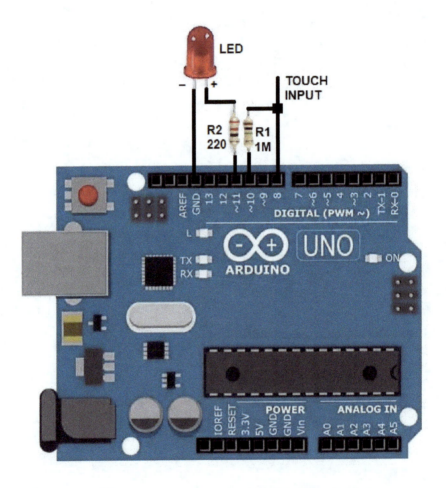

Figure 24: Capacitive Touch Sensor with PWM LED Out

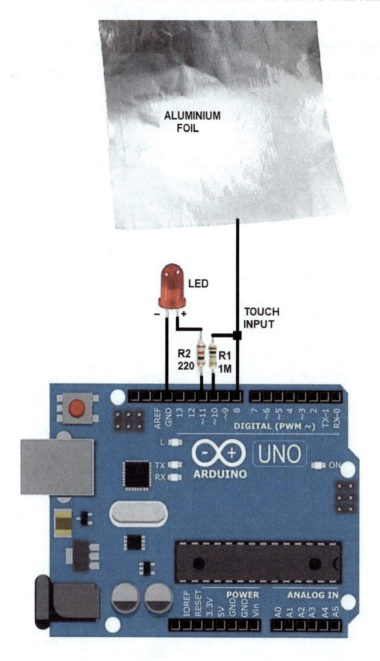

Figure 25: Aluminium Foil used as Touch Sensor Capacitive Input

10.1 Source Code to vary LED Brightness with Touch Distance from Aluminium Foil Connected to Capacitive Input

```
#define SensorOut 10
#define SensorIn 8
#define PWMPin 11
const int maximum = 300;
const int minimum = 12;

void setup() {
  pinMode(SensorOut, OUTPUT);
  pinMode(SensorIn, INPUT);
  pinMode(PWMPin, OUTPUT);
  Serial.begin(9600);
}

void loop() {
  digitalWrite(SensorOut, LOW);
  delay(10);
  long startTime = micros();
  digitalWrite(SensorOut, HIGH);
  while (digitalRead(SensorIn) == LOW);
  long sensorVal = micros() - startTime;
  Serial.println(sensorVal);
  analogWrite(PWMPin, map(sensorVal, 12, 300,
0, 255));
}
```

Listing 6: Capacitive Sensor to PWM LED Ouput

10.2 Explanation of Source Code

This program uses a similar structure as the previous program but converts the sensorVal with the Mapping function:

```
Serial.println(sensorVal);
analogWrite(PWMPin, map(sensorVal, 12, 300, 0, 255));
```

The PWM output ranges from 0 to 255, which is from OFF to Maximum brightness.

An Introduction to the Arduino Capacitive Sensor Library

The Capacitive Sensor Library turns two or more Arduino pins into a capacitive sensor, which can sense the electrical capacitance of the human body. All the sensor setup requires is a medium to high value resistor and a piece of wire and a small piece of aluminium foil on the end. At its most sensitive, the sensor will start to sense a hand or body inches away from the sensor.

The Capacitive Sensor Library was written by Paul Badger and further developed by Paul Stoffregen. The Library can be downloaded from:

https://www.arduinolibraries.info/libraries/capacitive-sensor

or the Zip file from:

https://downloads.arduino.cc/libraries/github.com/PaulStoffregen/CapacitiveSensor-0.5.1.zip

This library is compatible with all architectures so you should be able to use it on all the Arduino boards. To use this library, open the Library Manager in the Arduino IDE and install it from there:

https://www.arduino.cc/en/Guide/Libraries

11.1 Using Capacitive Sensor Library for a single Switch to Serial Out

```
#include <CapacitiveSensor.h>

/*
  Capacitive Sensor Library
  Paul Badger and Paul Stoffregen
  https://downloads.arduino.cc/libraries/github
.com/PaulStoffregen/CapacitiveSensor-0.5.1.zip
  Uses a high value resistor e.g. 10 megohm
between send pin and receive pin
  Resistor effects sensitivity, experiment with
values, 50 kilohm - 50 megohm. Larger resistor
values yield larger sensor values.
  Receive pin is the sensor pin - try different
amounts of foil/metal on this pin
  Best results are obtained if sensor foil and
wire is covered with an insulator such as paper
or plastic sheet
*/

CapacitiveSensor   cs_10_8 =
CapacitiveSensor(10, 8);        // 1 megohm
resistor between pins 10 & 8, pin 8 is sensor
pin

void setup()
{
  Serial.begin(9600);
}

void loop()
{
  long start = millis();
  long total1 =  cs_10_8.capacitiveSensor(20);

  Serial.print(millis() - start);        //
check on performance in milliseconds
  Serial.print("\t");                    // tab
```

```
character for debug window spacing

  Serial.println(total1);                        //
print sensor output 1
  Serial.print("\t");

  delay(10);                                       //
arbitrary delay to limit data to serial port
}
```

Listing 7: Capacitive Sensor Library for a single Switch to Serial Out

11.2 Explanation of Source Code

The Capacitive Sensor Library is called using:

```
#include <CapacitiveSensor.h>
```

The sensor is initialised by:

```
CapacitiveSensor   cs_10_8 = CapacitiveSensor(10,
8);        // 1 megohm resistor between pins 10 &
8, pin 8 is sensor pin
```

Pin 8 is now inialized as the Capacitive Sensor Touch Pin.

The Serial Output is set to run at 9600 Baud rate using:

```
  Serial.begin(9600);
```

The Main Loop saves the starting time in millis using:

```
  long start = millis();
```

The present touch value is calculated with:

```
long total1 =  cs_10_8.capacitiveSensor(20);
```

Then the Time and Touch values are printed to the screen using the Arduino Serial Print command:

```
Serial.print(millis() - start);        // check
on performance in milliseconds
Serial.print("\t");                     // tab
character for debug window spacing

Serial.println(total1);                 //
print sensor output 1
Serial.print("\t");
```

11.3 Using Capacitive Sensor Library for a dual Slider Switch to Serial Out

This program is designed to operate as a slider switch which can be used to increment or decrement a value. When either switch is touched the value is incremented or decremented by +1 or -1. However if either switch is touched for more than half a second then the value is rapidly incremented or decremented at a speed dependent on a programmed software delay value.

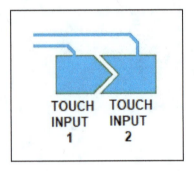

Picture 1: Dual Slider Switch Layout

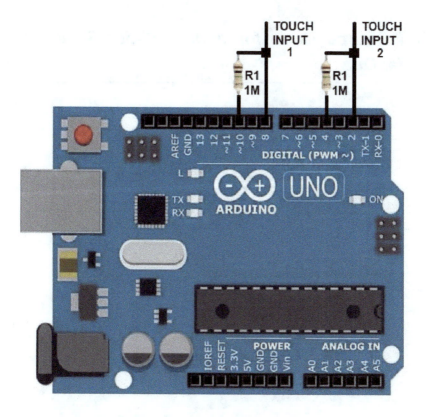

Figure 26: Connection Wiring for Dual Slider Switch

11.4 Source Code for a dual Slider Switch to Serial Out

```
#include <CapacitiveSensor.h>

/*
   Capacitive Sensor Library
   Paul Badger and Paul Stoffregen

  https://downloads.arduino.cc/libraries/github
.com/PaulStoffregen/CapacitiveSensor-0.5.1.zip
   Uses a high value resistor e.g. 10 megohm
between send pin and receive pin
   Resistor effects sensitivity, experiment
with values, 50 kilohm - 50 megohm. Larger
resistor values yield larger sensor values.
   Receive pin is the sensor pin - try
different amounts of foil/metal on this pin
   Best results are obtained if sensor foil and
wire is covered with an insulator such as paper
or plastic sheet
*/

#define switchCount 2   // number of switches

int n = 0;
int value = 0;

CapacitiveSensor   cs_10_8 =
CapacitiveSensor(10, 8);        // 1 megohm
resistor between pins 10 & 8, pin 8 is sensor
pin,
CapacitiveSensor   cs_4_2 = CapacitiveSensor(4,
2);        // 1 megohm resistor between pins 4 &
2, pin 2 is sensor pin,

int ThresholdOn = 150;
int ThresholdOff = 100;

int Flag[switchCount];
```

```
long start[switchCount];
long total[switchCount];
long nowTime;

void setup()
{
  Serial.begin(9600);
}

void loop()
{

  total[0] =  cs_10_8.capacitiveSensor(20);
  total[1] =  cs_4_2.capacitiveSensor(20);

  checkSwitch1();
  checkSwitch2();
}
//----------------------------------------

void  checkSwitch1() {

  if ((total[0] >= ThresholdOn) && (Flag[0] ==
LOW)) {
    start[0] = millis();
    value = value + 1;
    if ( value >=  127) {
      value = 127;
    }

    Serial.print("Value1:  ");
    Serial.println(value);
    do {
      total[0] =  cs_10_8.capacitiveSensor(20);
// read switch
      nowTime = millis() - start[0];
      if (nowTime >= 500) {
        value = value + 1;
        if ( value >=  127) {
          value = 127;
        }
        Serial.print("Value2:  ");
        Serial.println(value);
```

```
          delay(50);
      }
    } while (total[0] >= ThresholdOff);
    Flag[0] = HIGH;


  }

  if ((total[0] <= ThresholdOff) && (Flag[0] ==
HIGH)) {
    Flag[0] = LOW;
  }
}
//------------------------------------------

void  checkSwitch2() {

  if ((total[1] >= ThresholdOn) && (Flag[1] ==
LOW)) {
    start[1] = millis();
    value = value - 1;
    if ( value <=  0) {
      value = 0;
    }

    Serial.print("Value1:  ");
    Serial.println(value);
    do {
      total[1] =  cs_4_2.capacitiveSensor(20);
      nowTime = millis() - start[1];
      if (nowTime >= 500) {
        value = value - 1;
        if ( value <=  0) {
          value = 0;
        }
        Serial.print("Value2:  ");
        Serial.println(value);
        delay(50);
      }
    } while (total[1] >= ThresholdOff);
    Flag[1] = HIGH;


  }
```

```
  if ((total[1] <= ThresholdOff) && (Flag[1] ==
HIGH)) {
    Flag[1] = LOW;
  }
}
//---------------------------------------
```

Listing 8: Source Code for a dual Slider Switch to Serial Out

11.5 Explanation of Source Code

The Capacitive Sensor Library is called using:

```
#include <CapacitiveSensor.h>
```

The capacitive pins to be used are initialised:

```
CapacitiveSensor   cs_10_8 = CapacitiveSensor(10,
8);        // 1 megohm resistor between pins 10 &
8, pin 8 is sensor pin,
CapacitiveSensor   cs_4_2 = CapacitiveSensor(4,
2);        // 1 megohm resistor between pins 5 &
2, pin 2 is sensor pin,
```

In the main Loop the two switch input values are read:

```
total[0] =  cs_10_8.capacitiveSensor(20);
total[1] =  cs_4_2.capacitiveSensor(20);
```

Then the switch values are checked:

```
checkSwitch1();
checkSwitch2();
```

Check Switch 1 checks to see if Switch 1 is greater than the ThresholdOn value and that it is not already switched ON using the following logic. If the switch is pressed then the start time is saved from the millis() value and the value is incremented by +1 until the value reaches the maximum allowed value of 127.

```
if ((total[0] >= ThresholdOn) && (Flag[0] ==
LOW)) {
   start[0] = millis();
   value = value + 1;
   if ( value >=  127) {
     value = 127;
   }
```

Then the value is printed using:

```
Serial.print("Value1:   ");
Serial.println(value);
```

Then a **DO WHILE** Loop is implemented, where the switch is read while the switch is greater or equal to the ThresholdOff value. Within this Loop the value is incremented and finally printed to the Serial port:

```
do {
   total[0] =  cs_10_8.capacitiveSensor(20);
// read switch
   nowTime = millis() - start[0];
   if (nowTime >= 500) {
     value = value + 1;
     if ( value >=  127) {
       value = 127;
     }
     Serial.print("Value2:   ");
     Serial.println(value);
     delay(50);
   }
} while (total[0] >= ThresholdOff);
```

Then after leaving the DO WHILE Loop if the total[0] is less than the ThresholdOff value then the Flag[0] is cleared to LOW:

```
if ((total[0] <= ThresholdOff) && (Flag[0] ==
HIGH)) {
    Flag[0] = LOW;
```

The Check Switch 2 function works in a similar manner except the value is decremented by -1 steps to a minimum of zero.

11.6 Source Code for a dual Slider Switch to MIDI Volume Control Change Command Out

```cpp
#include <CapacitiveSensor.h>
#include <MIDI.h>

MIDI_CREATE_DEFAULT_INSTANCE();

#define switchCount 2   // number of switches

int n = 0;
int value = 0;     // Initial value
int volume = 7;    // MIDI Volume Command Number
int channel = 1;   // MIDI Channel 1

CapacitiveSensor   cs_10_8 =
CapacitiveSensor(10, 8);        // 1 megohm
resistor between pins 10 & 8, pin 8 is sensor
pin,
CapacitiveSensor   cs_4_2 = CapacitiveSensor(4,
2);         // 1 megohm resistor between pins 4 &
2, pin 2 is sensor pin,

int ThresholdOn = 150;
int ThresholdOff = 100;

int Flag[switchCount];
long start[switchCount];
long total[switchCount];
long nowTime;

void setup()
{
  MIDI.begin(MIDI_CHANNEL_OMNI);
}

void loop()
{
```

```
  total[0] =   cs_10_8.capacitiveSensor(20);
  total[1] =   cs_4_2.capacitiveSensor(20);

  checkSwitch1();
  checkSwitch2();
}
//-----------------------------------------

void  checkSwitch1() {

  if ((total[0] >= ThresholdOn) && (Flag[0] ==
LOW)) {
    start[0] = millis();
    value = value + 1;
    if ( value >=  127) {
      value = 127;
    }
    MIDI.sendControlChange(volume, value,
channel);
    do {
      total[0] =   cs_10_8.capacitiveSensor(20);
// read switch
      nowTime = millis() - start[0];
      if (nowTime >= 500) {
        value = value + 1;
        if ( value >=  127) {
          value = 127;
        }
        MIDI.sendControlChange(volume, value,
channel);
        delay(50);
      }
    } while (total[0] >= ThresholdOff);
    Flag[0] = HIGH;

  }

  if ((total[0] <= ThresholdOff) && (Flag[0] ==
HIGH)) {
    Flag[0] = LOW;
  }
}
//-----------------------------------------
```

```
void  checkSwitch2() {

  if ((total[1] >= ThresholdOn) && (Flag[1] ==
LOW)) {
     start[1] = millis();
     value = value - 1;
     if ( value <=  0) {
       value = 0;
     }
     MIDI.sendControlChange(volume, value,
channel);
     do {
        total[1] =  cs_4_2.capacitiveSensor(20);
        nowTime = millis() - start[1];
        if (nowTime >= 500) {
          value = value - 1;
          if ( value <=  0) {
             value = 0;
          }
          MIDI.sendControlChange(volume, value,
channel);
          delay(50);
        }
     } while (total[1] >= ThresholdOff);
     Flag[1] = HIGH;

  }

  if ((total[1] <= ThresholdOff) && (Flag[1] ==
HIGH)) {
     Flag[1] = LOW;
  }
}
```

Listing 9: Dual Slider Switch for MIDI Volume Control Change Out

11.7 Explanation of the Source Code

The Capacitive Sensor Library is called using:

```
#include <CapacitiveSensor.h>
```

The capacitive pins to be used are initialised:

```
CapacitiveSensor   cs_10_8 = CapacitiveSensor(10,
8);        // 1 megohm resistor between pins 10 &
8, pin 8 is sensor pin,
CapacitiveSensor   cs_4_2 = CapacitiveSensor(4,
2);          // 1 megohm resistor between pins 5 &
2, pin 2 is sensor pin,
```

The source code uses the MIDI Library:

```
//https://www.arduino.cc/reference/en/libraries/midi-library/

#include <MIDI.h>
MIDI_CREATE_DEFAULT_INSTANCE();
```

MIDI commands are initialized by:

```
  MIDI.begin(MIDI_CHANNEL_OMNI);
```

The rest of the program functions in a similar way to the previous program except instead of outputting the data to the Serial Port it is transmitted to the MIDI Output using:

```
        MIDI.sendControlChange(volume, value,
channel);
```

where the value, volume and channel are inialized to:

```
int value = 0;     // Initial value
int volume = 7;    // MIDI Volume Command Number
int channel = 1;   // MIDI Channel 1
```

Note that the MIDI Volume value can range from 0 to 127.

A Capacitive Touch Encoder using an Arduino Screw Shield Board

The Arduino Uno Screw Shield board is available from many sources. It plugs directly into the Arduino Uno board and connects all the pins to the screw terminals. Also it provides a matrix board to which the required resistors can be soldered, for the touch capacitor inputs. This allows the screw terminal connectors to be connected to external conductive objects to produce a MIDI music instrument output.

Figure 27: A Screw Shield Board mounted on an Arduino Uno Board

12.1 Operation

The MIDI Channel is preset to MIDI Channel 1. However other values for the MIDI Channel and the note range can be pre-programmed into the firmware. This unit can work in the standard MIDI Baud rate of 31250.

12.2 Features

The 13 Note Screw Shield Touch Sensor to Serial Out Unit consists of an a MIDI Arduino Uno Board, a 2.1mm power socket, and associated power LED, a 9v battery or equivalent DC power source or powered via the USB socket and 13 1M ohm resistors for the Touch Inputs.

12.3 Source Code for a 13 Input Screw Shield Touch Sensor to Serial Out

```
#include <CapacitiveSensor.h>

#define noteCount 13  // number of notes used
in the note range

CapacitiveSensor   cs_12_14 =
CapacitiveSensor(12, 14);
CapacitiveSensor   cs_12_15 =
CapacitiveSensor(12, 15);
CapacitiveSensor   cs_12_16 =
CapacitiveSensor(12, 16);
CapacitiveSensor   cs_12_17 =
CapacitiveSensor(12, 17);
CapacitiveSensor   cs_19_18 =
CapacitiveSensor(19, 18);
CapacitiveSensor   cs_2_3 = CapacitiveSensor(2,
3);
CapacitiveSensor   cs_2_4 = CapacitiveSensor(2,
4);
CapacitiveSensor   cs_2_5 = CapacitiveSensor(2,
5);
CapacitiveSensor   cs_2_6 = CapacitiveSensor(2,
6);
CapacitiveSensor   cs_7_8 = CapacitiveSensor(7,
8);
CapacitiveSensor   cs_7_9 = CapacitiveSensor(7,
9);
CapacitiveSensor   cs_7_10 =
CapacitiveSensor(7, 10);
CapacitiveSensor   cs_7_11 =
CapacitiveSensor(7, 11);

int note[13] = {
```

```
   0, 1, 2, 3, 4, 5, 6, 7, 8, 9, 10, 11, 12
};

int ThresholdOn = 150;
int ThresholdOff = 100;
int MIDIchannel = 1;
int startNote = 48; // C below middle C
int Flag[noteCount];
long start[noteCount];
long total[noteCount];
int n = 0;

//----------------------------------------
void setup()
{
  Serial.begin(9600);

  for (int x = 0; x < noteCount; x++) {
    Flag[noteCount] = 0;
  }
}

//----------------------------------------

void loop()
{
  total[0] =  cs_12_14.capacitiveSensor(20);
  total[1] =  cs_12_15.capacitiveSensor(20);
  total[2] =  cs_12_16.capacitiveSensor(20);
  total[3] =  cs_12_17.capacitiveSensor(20);
  total[4] =  cs_19_18.capacitiveSensor(20);
  total[5] =  cs_2_3.capacitiveSensor(20);
  total[6] =  cs_2_4.capacitiveSensor(20);
  total[7] =  cs_2_5.capacitiveSensor(20);
  total[8] =  cs_2_6.capacitiveSensor(20);
  total[9] =  cs_7_8.capacitiveSensor(20);
  total[10] =  cs_7_9.capacitiveSensor(20);
  total[11] =  cs_7_10.capacitiveSensor(20);
  total[12] =  cs_7_11.capacitiveSensor(20);

  for (n = 0; n < noteCount; n++) {

    if ((total[n] >= ThresholdOn) && (Flag[n]
```

```
== LOW)) {
      Serial.print("INPUT:   ");
      Serial.println(n);
      Serial.print("Threshold On:   ");
      Serial.println(total[n]);
      Flag[n] = HIGH;
    }

    if ((total[n] < ThresholdOff) && (Flag[n]
== HIGH)) {
      Serial.print("INPUT:   ");
      Serial.println(n);
      Serial.print("Threshold Off:   ");
      Serial.println(total[n]);
      Flag[n] = LOW;
    }
  }
}
//---------------------------------
```

Listing 10: Code for 13 Input Screw Shield to Serial Out

12.4 Explanation of the Source Code

The Capacitive Sensor Library is called using:

```
#include <CapacitiveSensor.h>
```

The 13 Capacitive touch inputs are initialised by:

```
CapacitiveSensor   cs_12_14 =
CapacitiveSensor(12, 14);
CapacitiveSensor   cs_12_15 =
CapacitiveSensor(12, 15);
CapacitiveSensor   cs_12_16 =
CapacitiveSensor(12, 16);
```

```
CapacitiveSensor   cs_12_17 =
CapacitiveSensor(12, 17);
CapacitiveSensor   cs_19_18 =
CapacitiveSensor(19, 18);
CapacitiveSensor   cs_2_3 = CapacitiveSensor(2,
3);
CapacitiveSensor   cs_2_4 = CapacitiveSensor(2,
4);
CapacitiveSensor   cs_2_5 = CapacitiveSensor(2,
5);
CapacitiveSensor   cs_2_6 = CapacitiveSensor(2,
6);
CapacitiveSensor   cs_7_8 = CapacitiveSensor(7,
8);
CapacitiveSensor   cs_7_9 = CapacitiveSensor(7,
9);
CapacitiveSensor   cs_7_10 = CapacitiveSensor(7,
10);
CapacitiveSensor   cs_7_11 = CapacitiveSensor(7,
11);
```

The 13 Note value Offsets are stored in the array:

```
int note[13] = {
  0, 1, 2, 3, 4, 5, 6, 7, 8, 9, 10, 11, 12
};
```

The variables and constants are initialised:

```
int ThresholdOn = 150;
int ThresholdOff = 100;
int MIDIchannel = 1;
int startNote = 48; // C below middle C
int Flag[noteCount];
long start[noteCount];
long total[noteCount];
int n = 0;
```

In the Setup routine the Serial port is initialized to 9600 Baud and the Flags are inialized to zero:

```
Serial.begin(9600);
```

```
for (int x = 0; x < noteCount; x++) {
  Flag[noteCount] = 0;
}
```

In the main Loop routine the 13 switches are read:

```
total[0]  =  cs_12_14.capacitiveSensor(20);
total[1]  =  cs_12_15.capacitiveSensor(20);
total[2]  =  cs_12_16.capacitiveSensor(20);
total[3]  =  cs_12_17.capacitiveSensor(20);
total[4]  =  cs_19_18.capacitiveSensor(20);
total[5]  =  cs_2_3.capacitiveSensor(20);
total[6]  =  cs_2_4.capacitiveSensor(20);
total[7]  =  cs_2_5.capacitiveSensor(20);
total[8]  =  cs_2_6.capacitiveSensor(20);
total[9]  =  cs_7_8.capacitiveSensor(20);
total[10] =  cs_7_9.capacitiveSensor(20);
total[11] =  cs_7_10.capacitiveSensor(20);
total[12] =  cs_7_11.capacitiveSensor(20);
```

Then the FOR Loop reads the value of the 13 switches and Serial Prints their values depending on the ThresholdOn, ThresholdOFF and the Flag[n] values:

```
for (n = 0; n < noteCount; n++) {

    if ((total[n] >= ThresholdOn) && (Flag[n] ==
LOW)) {
        Serial.print("INPUT:  ");
        Serial.println(n);
        Serial.print("Threshold On:  ");
        Serial.println(total[n]);
        Flag[n] = HIGH;
    }

    if ((total[n] < ThresholdOff) && (Flag[n] ==
HIGH)) {
        Serial.print("INPUT:  ");
        Serial.println(n);
        Serial.print("Threshold Off:  ");
        Serial.println(total[n]);
```

```
      Flag[n] = LOW;
    }
  }
}
```

12.5 Arduino Screw Shield 13 Input Connections

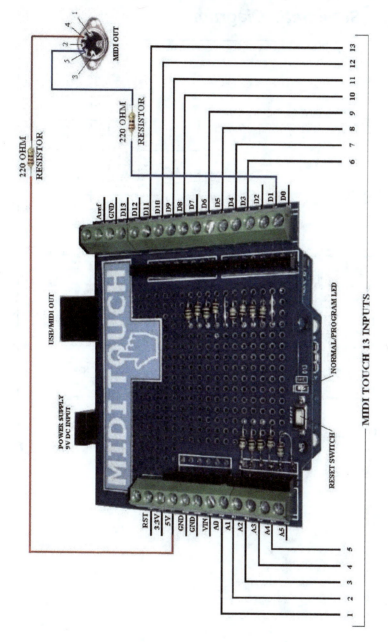

Figure 28: Arduino Screw Shield MIDI Touch 13 Inputs Connections

12.6 The Arduino Screw Shield 13 Input Touch Switch Schematic Diagram

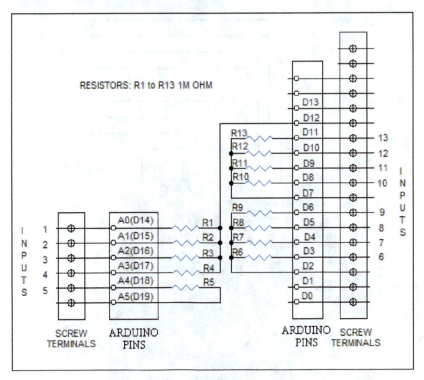

Figure 29: Arduino Screw Shield 13 Input Touch Switch Schematic

12.7 *Wiring layout for 13 Input Touch Controller*

The 13 1M Ohm resistors are soldered and wired on the Arduino Screw shield board as shown below:

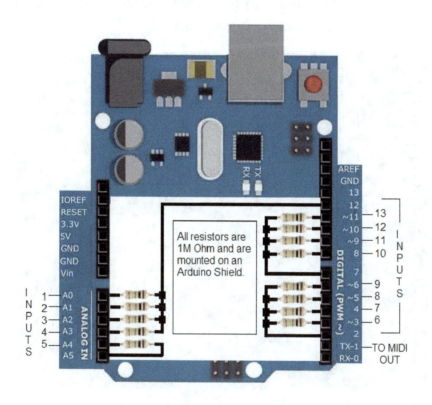

Figure 30: Wiring Layout for 13 Input Touch Controller

A 13 Note MIDI Fruit Piano

The screw terminal connectors of the previous 13 input Screw Shield project can be connected to various external conductive objects to produce a MIDI music instrument output. The material of the touch object only has to be slightly conductive, so plants, fruit, vegetables and water can also work!

Picture 2: MIDI Fruit Piano

13.1 Operation

This project uses different fruits wired and connected to the Screw Terminal Touch Inputs. The fruit can be connected using wires connected to alligator type clips. A video demonstration of the operation of the fruit MIDI Touch Interfaces is available at: https://www.youtube.com/watch?v=C3Q2fN3JH7Y&t=18s

13.2 Features

The 13 Note Fruit Screw Shield Touch Sensor to MIDI Out Unit consists of an a MIDI Arduino Uno Board, the MIDI channel is preset to channel 1, the velocity byte is preset to a value of 100, a 2.1mm power socket, and associated power LED, a MIDI 5-pin DIN output socket and associated series resistors, a 9v battery or equivalent DC power source or powered via the USB socket and 13 1M ohm resistors for the Touch Inputs.

13.3 Source Code for a 13 Note Fruit Touch Sensor to MIDI Out

```
#include <CapacitiveSensor.h>
#include <MIDI.h>

MIDI_CREATE_DEFAULT_INSTANCE();

#define noteCount 13  // number of notes used
in the note range

CapacitiveSensor   cs_12_14 =
CapacitiveSensor(12, 14);
CapacitiveSensor   cs_12_15 =
CapacitiveSensor(12, 15);
CapacitiveSensor   cs_12_16 =
CapacitiveSensor(12, 16);
CapacitiveSensor   cs_12_17 =
CapacitiveSensor(12, 17);
CapacitiveSensor   cs_19_18 =
CapacitiveSensor(19, 18);
CapacitiveSensor   cs_2_3 = CapacitiveSensor(2,
3);
CapacitiveSensor   cs_2_4 = CapacitiveSensor(2,
4);
CapacitiveSensor   cs_2_5 = CapacitiveSensor(2,
5);
CapacitiveSensor   cs_2_6 = CapacitiveSensor(2,
6);
```

```
CapacitiveSensor    cs_7_8 = CapacitiveSensor(7,
8);
CapacitiveSensor    cs_7_9 = CapacitiveSensor(7,
9);
CapacitiveSensor    cs_7_10 =
CapacitiveSensor(7, 10);
CapacitiveSensor    cs_7_11 =
CapacitiveSensor(7, 11);

int note[13] = {
  0, 1, 2, 3, 4, 5, 6, 7, 8, 9, 10, 11, 12
};

int ThresholdOn = 150;
int ThresholdOff = 100;   //60;
int MIDIchannel = 1;
int startNote = 48; // C below middle C
int Flag[noteCount];
long total[noteCount];
int n = 0;

//-----------------------------------
void setup()
{
  MIDI.begin(MIDI_CHANNEL_OMNI);
  MIDI.turnThruOn();

  for (int x = 0; x < noteCount; x++) {
    Flag[noteCount] = 0;
  }
}

//-----------------------------------

void loop()
{
  total[0] =  cs_12_14.capacitiveSensor(20);
  total[1] =  cs_12_15.capacitiveSensor(20);
  total[2] =  cs_12_16.capacitiveSensor(20);
  total[3] =  cs_12_17.capacitiveSensor(20);
  total[4] =  cs_19_18.capacitiveSensor(20);
  total[5] =  cs_2_3.capacitiveSensor(20);
  total[6] =  cs_2_4.capacitiveSensor(20);
```

```
    total[7]  =   cs_2_5.capacitiveSensor(20);
    total[8]  =   cs_2_6.capacitiveSensor(20);
    total[9]  =   cs_7_8.capacitiveSensor(20);
    total[10]  =   cs_7_9.capacitiveSensor(20);
    total[11]  =   cs_7_10.capacitiveSensor(20);
    total[12]  =   cs_7_11.capacitiveSensor(20);

    for (n = 0; n < noteCount; n++) {

        if ((total[n] >= ThresholdOn) && (Flag[n]
== LOW)) {
            MIDI.sendNoteOn(note[n] + startNote, 100,
MIDIchannel); // Send a Note (pitch, velocity
100 on MIDI channel )
            Flag[n] = HIGH;
        }

        if ((total[n] < ThresholdOff) && (Flag[n]
== HIGH)) {
            MIDI.sendNoteOff(note[n] + startNote,
100, MIDIchannel);
            Flag[n] = LOW;
        }
    }
}
//-----------------------------------
```

Listing 11: Source code for Fruit Touch Sensor to MIDI

13.4 Explanation of Source Code

The source code is similar to the previous project except the data is transmitted to the MIDI Out port.

The source code uses the MIDI Library:

//https://www.arduino.cc/reference/en/libraries/m
idi-library/

#include <MIDI.h>

```
MIDI_CREATE_DEFAULT_INSTANCE();
```

MIDI commands are initialized by:

```
MIDI.begin(MIDI_CHANNEL_OMNI);
```

In the FOR Loop if the total[n] is greater or equal to the ThresholdOn AND the Flag[n] is LOW then a corresponding MIDI Note On is transmittted, and the Flag[n] is set HIGH:

```
    if ((total[n] >= ThresholdOn) && (Flag[n] ==
LOW)) {
        MIDI.sendNoteOn(note[n] + startNote, 100,
MIDIchannel); // Send a Note (pitch, velocity 100
on MIDI channel )
        Flag[n] = HIGH;
```

Also in the FOR Loop if the total[n] is less than or equal to the ThresholdOff AND the Flag[n] is HIGH then a corresponding MIDI Note Off is transmittted, and the Flag[n] is cleared to LOW:

```
    if ((total[n] < ThresholdOff) && (Flag[n] ==
HIGH)) {
        MIDI.sendNoteOff(note[n] + startNote, 100,
MIDIchannel);
        Flag[n] = LOW;
    }
```

13.5 MIDI Out Schematic circuit diagram for the 13 Note Fruit Touch Inputs

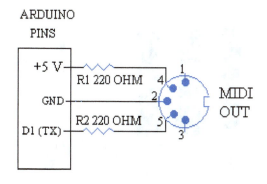

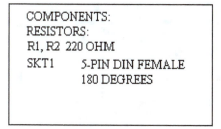

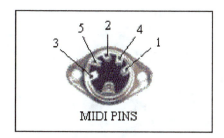

Figure 31: MIDI Out Schematic for the 13 Note Fruit Touch Encoder

13.6 Layout for a 13 Note Keyboard

It is possible to use the 13 Note Touch Inputs for a simple MIDI Keyboard Encoder:

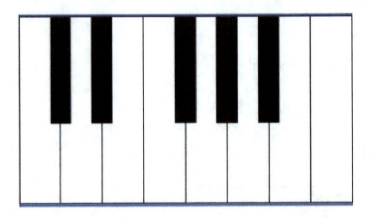

Picture 3: Layout of 13 Notes Keyboard

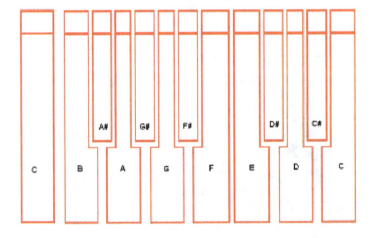

Picture 4: Reverse Layout of the back of 13 Notes Keyboard

A Simple MIDI 8 Note Touch Xylophone Encoder

This design is an example of how to implement a MIDI 8 Note Xylophone using an 8 input Capacitive Touch Sensor arrangement. Since paint can be an insulator you may need to scrape off some paint from underneath the xylophone bars to make good contact to the touch controller connecting wires.

Picture 5: 8 Note Xylophone

14.1 Features

The MIDI 8 Note Touch Xylophone Encoder consists of of a MIDI Arduino Uno Board, the velocity byte is preset to a value of 100, the MIDI channel is set to channel 1 for all the touch switches, a 2.1mm power socket, and associated power LED, a MIDI 5-pin DIN output socket and associated series resistors, the unit requires a 9v battery or equivalent DC power source or it can be powered via the USB socket.

14.2 Operation

Generally Xylophones are played with very hard rubber, wooden-headed or acrylic mallets. However the mallets need to be covered in a conductive material so the hands can produce the capacitive touch to trigger the MIDI 8 Note Xylophone. One solution is to use adhesive-backed copper tape to cover the mallet and handle.

Picture 6: Mallets with one covered by adhesive-backed copper tape

14.3 Source Code for the MIDI 8 Note Touch Xylophone Encoder

```
#include <CapacitiveSensor.h>
#include <MIDI.h>

#define note1 60   // Start Note Middle C to
match Xylophone
#define note2 62
#define note3 64
#define note4 65
#define note5 67
#define note6 69
#define note7 71
#define note8 72

#define programChangeNum 13 // Xylophone

MIDI_CREATE_DEFAULT_INSTANCE();

#define notes 8   // number of notes

CapacitiveSensor   cs_12_14 =
CapacitiveSensor(12, 14);
CapacitiveSensor   cs_12_15 =
CapacitiveSensor(12, 15);
CapacitiveSensor   cs_12_16 =
CapacitiveSensor(12, 16);
CapacitiveSensor   cs_12_17 =
CapacitiveSensor(12, 17);
CapacitiveSensor   cs_19_18 =
CapacitiveSensor(19, 18);
CapacitiveSensor   cs_2_3 = CapacitiveSensor(2,
3);
CapacitiveSensor   cs_2_4 = CapacitiveSensor(2,
4);
CapacitiveSensor   cs_2_5 = CapacitiveSensor(2,
5);
```

```
int noteType[8] = {
  note1, note2, note3, note4, note5, note6,
note7, note8
};

int ThresholdOn = 150;
int ThresholdOff = 100;
int MIDIchannel = 1;   // Channel 1
int Octave = 12;
int Flag[notes];
long total[notes];
int n = 0;

//-------------------------------------
void setup()
{
  MIDI.begin(MIDI_CHANNEL_OMNI);
  MIDI.turnThruOn();

  for (int x = 0; x < notes; x++) {
    Flag[notes] = 0;
  }
  MIDI.sendProgramChange(programChangeNum,
MIDIchannel);
}
//-------------------------------------

void loop()
{
  total[0] =  cs_12_14.capacitiveSensor(20);
  total[1] =  cs_12_15.capacitiveSensor(20);
  total[2] =  cs_12_16.capacitiveSensor(20);
  total[3] =  cs_12_17.capacitiveSensor(20);
  total[4] =  cs_19_18.capacitiveSensor(20);
  total[5] =  cs_2_3.capacitiveSensor(20);
  total[6] =  cs_2_4.capacitiveSensor(20);
  total[7] =  cs_2_5.capacitiveSensor(20);


  for (n = 0; n < notes; n++) {

    if ((total[n] >= ThresholdOn) && (Flag[n]
== LOW)) {
```

```
        MIDI.sendNoteOn(noteType[n] + Octave,
100, MIDIchannel);
        Flag[n] = HIGH;
    }

    if ((total[n] < ThresholdOff) && (Flag[n]
== HIGH)) {
        MIDI.sendNoteOff(noteType[n] + Octave,
100, MIDIchannel);
        Flag[n] = LOW;
    }
  }
}
//--------------------------------
```

Listing 12: Code for a MIDI 8 Note Touch Xylophone Encoder

14.4 Explanation of the Source Code

The Capacitive Sensor Library is called using:

```
#include <CapacitiveSensor.h>
```

The source code uses the MIDI Library:

```
//https://www.arduino.cc/reference/en/libraries/m
idi-library/
```

```
#include <MIDI.h>
MIDI_CREATE_DEFAULT_INSTANCE();
```

MIDI commands are initialized by:

```
  MIDI.begin(MIDI_CHANNEL_OMNI);
```

The 8 Note scale is initialized by:

```
#define note1 60  // Start Note Middle C to match
Xylophone
#define note2 62
#define note3 64
#define note4 65
```

```
#define note5 67
#define note6 69
#define note7 71
#define note8 72
```

The 8 Note Touch Inupts are initialized by:

```
CapacitiveSensor   cs_12_14 =
CapacitiveSensor(12, 14);
CapacitiveSensor   cs_12_15 =
CapacitiveSensor(12, 15);
CapacitiveSensor   cs_12_16 =
CapacitiveSensor(12, 16);
CapacitiveSensor   cs_12_17 =
CapacitiveSensor(12, 17);
CapacitiveSensor   cs_19_18 =
CapacitiveSensor(19, 18);
CapacitiveSensor   cs_2_3 = CapacitiveSensor(2,
3);
CapacitiveSensor   cs_2_4 = CapacitiveSensor(2,
4);
CapacitiveSensor   cs_2_5 = CapacitiveSensor(2,
5);
```

The Variables and Constants are inialized by:

```
int noteType[8] = {
  note1, note2, note3, note4, note5, note6,
note7, note8
};

int ThresholdOn = 150;
int ThresholdOff = 100;
int MIDIchannel = 1;   // Channel 1
int Octave = 12;
int Flag[notes];
long total[notes];
int n = 0;
```

The Setup routine inializes MIDI, sets the Flags to zero and sends a MID Program Change to select a Xylophone sound:

```
MIDI.begin(MIDI_CHANNEL_OMNI);
MIDI.turnThruOn();

for (int x = 0; x < notes; x++) {
  Flag[notes] = 0;
}
MIDI.sendProgramChange(programChangeNum,
MIDIchannel);
```

In the main program Loop routine the 8 switch inputs are read:

```
total[0] =  cs_12_14.capacitiveSensor(20);
total[1] =  cs_12_15.capacitiveSensor(20);
total[2] =  cs_12_16.capacitiveSensor(20);
total[3] =  cs_12_17.capacitiveSensor(20);
total[4] =  cs_19_18.capacitiveSensor(20);
total[5] =  cs_2_3.capacitiveSensor(20);
total[6] =  cs_2_4.capacitiveSensor(20);
total[7] =  cs_2_5.capacitiveSensor(20);
```

In the FOR Loop if the total[n] is greater or equal to the ThresholdOn AND the Flag[n] is LOW then a corresponding MIDI Note On is transmittted, and the Flag[n] is set HIGH:

```
if ((total[n] >= ThresholdOn) && (Flag[n] ==
LOW)) {
    MIDI.sendNoteOn(noteType[n] + Octave, 100,
MIDIchannel);
    Flag[n] = HIGH;
```

Also in the FOR Loop if the total[n] is less than or equal to the ThresholdOff AND the Flag[n] is HIGH then a corresponding MIDI Note Off is transmittted, and the Flag[n] is cleared to LOW:

```
if ((total[n] < ThresholdOff) && (Flag[n] ==
HIGH)) {
    MIDI.sendNoteOff(noteType[n] + Octave, 100,
MIDIchannel);
    Flag[n] = LOW;
  }
```

The Note transmitted has the Variable Octave = 12 added to it. So the program sounds an octave higher.

14.5 Wiring Layout for an 8 Note MIDI Touch Xylophone

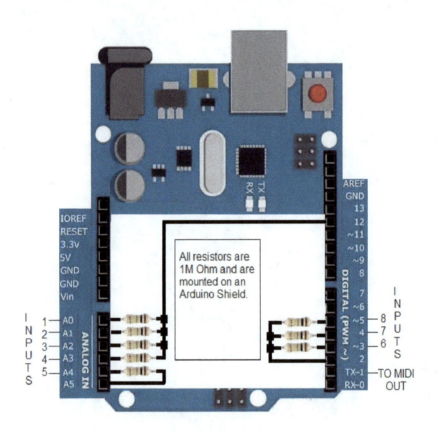

All resistors are 1M Ohm and are mounted on an Arduino Shield.

Figure 32: Wiring Layout for 8 Note MIDI Touch Xylophone

14.6 Circuit Schematic diagram for 8 Note MIDI Touch Xylophone

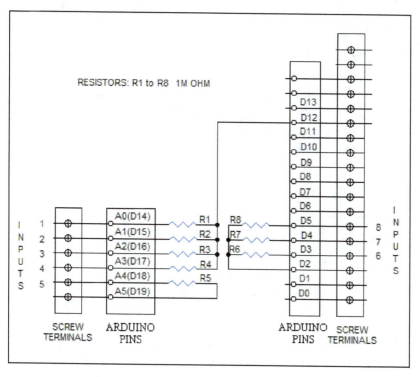

Figure 33: Circuit Schematic diagram for 8 Note MIDI Touch Xylophone

14.7 MIDI Out Circuit Schematic diagram for the 8 Note MIDI Xylophone

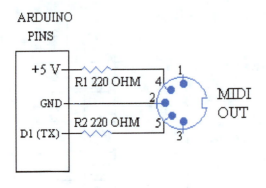

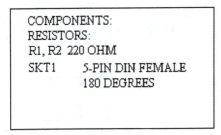

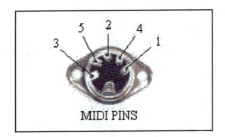

Figure 34: Circuit Schematic diagram for MIDI Out

14.8 Layout and Notes of 8-Way Xylophone

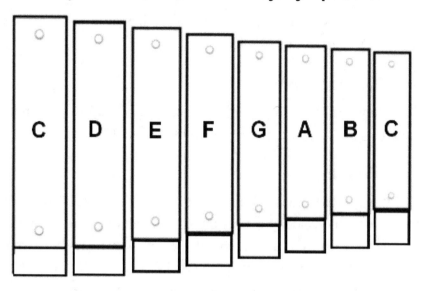

Picture 7: Layout and Notes of 8-Way Xylophone

A 9-Way MIDI Touch Drum Kit Encoder

This project uses capacitive touch sensor inputs to produce a 9-way MIDI touch drum encoder.

15.1 Operation

The drums can be arranged in a typical drum setup using copper tape on paper and then can be played using your fingers.

15.2 Features

The 9-way MIDI Touch drum kit consists of of a MIDI Arduino Uno Board, the velocity byte is preset to a value of 100, the MIDI channel is set to channel 1 for all the touch switches, a 2.1mm power socket, and associated power LED, a MIDI 5-pin DIN output socket and associated series resistors, the unit requires a 9v battery or equivalent DC power source or it can be powered via the USB socket.

15.3 Source Code for the 9-Way MIDI Touch Drum Kit Encoder

```
#include <CapacitiveSensor.h>
#include <MIDI.h>

/***********************************************
  // General MIDI (GM) Drum Selections
  35 Bass Kick; 36 Rock Kick; 37 Side Kick; 38
Acoustic Snare;
  39 Handclap; 40 Electric Snare; 41 Low Floor
Tom; 42 Closed Hi-Hat;
  43 High Floor Tom; 44 Pedal Hi-Hat; 45 Low
Tom; 46 Open Hi-Hat;
  47 Low Mid-Tom; 48 High Mid-Tom; 49 Crash
Cymbal 1; 50 High Tom
  51 Ride Cymbal 1; 52 Chinese Cymbal; 53 Ride
Bell; 54 Tambourine
```

```
   55 Splash Cymbal; 56 Cowbell; 57 Crash Cymbal
2; 58 Vibraslap
   59 Ride Cymbal 2; 60 High Bongo; 61 Low
Bongo; 62 Mute High Conga
   63 Open High Conga; 64 Low Conga; 65 High
Timbale; 66 Low Timbale
   67 High Agogo; 68 Low Agogo; 69 Cabasa; 70
Maracas; 71 Short Whistle
   72 Long Whistle; 73 Short Guiro; 74 Long
Guiro; 75 Claves; 76 High Woodblock
   77 Low Woodblock; 78 Mute Cuica; 79 Open
Cuico
   80 Mute Triangle; 81 Open Triangle
**********************************************/

#define drum1 42
#define drum2 35
#define drum3 38
#define drum4 49
#define drum5 50
#define drum6 43
#define drum7 47
#define drum8 51
#define drum9 60

MIDI_CREATE_DEFAULT_INSTANCE();

#define drums 9  // number of drums

CapacitiveSensor    cs_12_14 =
CapacitiveSensor(12, 14);
CapacitiveSensor    cs_12_15 =
CapacitiveSensor(12, 15);
CapacitiveSensor    cs_12_16 =
CapacitiveSensor(12, 16);
CapacitiveSensor    cs_12_17 =
CapacitiveSensor(12, 17);
CapacitiveSensor    cs_19_18 =
CapacitiveSensor(19, 18);
CapacitiveSensor    cs_2_3 = CapacitiveSensor(2,
3);
CapacitiveSensor    cs_2_4 = CapacitiveSensor(2,
4);
```

```
CapacitiveSensor    cs_2_5 = CapacitiveSensor(2,
5);
CapacitiveSensor    cs_2_6 = CapacitiveSensor(2,
6);
CapacitiveSensor    cs_7_8 = CapacitiveSensor(7,
8);
CapacitiveSensor    cs_7_9 = CapacitiveSensor(7,
9);
CapacitiveSensor    cs_7_10 =
CapacitiveSensor(7, 10);
CapacitiveSensor    cs_7_11 =
CapacitiveSensor(7, 11);

int drumType[9] = {
  drum1, drum2, drum3, drum4, drum5, drum6,
drum7, drum8, drum9
};

int ThresholdOn = 150;
int ThresholdOff = 100;   //60;
int MIDIchannel = 10;   // GM Drum Channel
int startdrumType = 48; // C below middle C
int Flag[drums];
long total[drums];
int n = 0;

//---------------------------------------
void setup()
{
  MIDI.begin(MIDI_CHANNEL_OMNI);
  MIDI.turnThruOn();

  for (int x = 0; x < drums; x++) {
    Flag[drums] = 0;
  }
}

//---------------------------------------

void loop()
{
  total[0] =  cs_12_14.capacitiveSensor(20);
  total[1] =  cs_12_15.capacitiveSensor(20);
```

```
   total[2]  =   cs_12_16.capacitiveSensor(20);
   total[3]  =   cs_12_17.capacitiveSensor(20);
   total[4]  =   cs_19_18.capacitiveSensor(20);
   total[5]  =   cs_2_3.capacitiveSensor(20);
   total[6]  =   cs_2_4.capacitiveSensor(20);
   total[7]  =   cs_2_5.capacitiveSensor(20);
   total[8]  =   cs_2_6.capacitiveSensor(20);
   total[9]  =   cs_7_8.capacitiveSensor(20);
   total[10] =   cs_7_9.capacitiveSensor(20);
   total[11] =   cs_7_10.capacitiveSensor(20);
   total[12] =   cs_7_11.capacitiveSensor(20);

   for (n = 0; n < drums; n++) {

      if ((total[n] >= ThresholdOn) && (Flag[n]
== LOW)) {
         MIDI.sendNoteOn(drumType[n], 100,
MIDIchannel);
         Flag[n] = HIGH;
      }

      if ((total[n] < ThresholdOff) && (Flag[n]
== HIGH)) {
         MIDI.sendNoteOff(drumType[n], 100,
MIDIchannel);
         Flag[n] = LOW;
      }
   }
}
//----------------------------------
```

Listing 13: 9-Way MIDI Touch Drum Encoder

15.4 Explanation of the Source Code

The source code uses the MIDI Library:

```
//https://www.arduino.cc/reference/en/libraries/m
idi-library/

#include <MIDI.h>
MIDI_CREATE_DEFAULT_INSTANCE();
```

The drum selections are set using:

```
#define drum1 42
#define drum2 35
#define drum3 38
#define drum4 49
#define drum5 50
#define drum6 43
#define drum7 47
#define drum8 51
#define drum9 60
```

The 9 input switches are set up starting with:

```
CapacitiveSensor   cs_12_14 =
CapacitiveSensor(12, 14);
```

The Variables and Constants are set up using:

```
int drumType[9] = {
  drum1, drum2, drum3, drum4, drum5, drum6,
drum7, drum8, drum9
};

int ThresholdOn = 150;
int ThresholdOff = 100;   //60;
int MIDIchannel = 10;   // GM Drum Channel
int startdrumType = 48; // C below middle C
int Flag[drums];
long total[drums];
int n = 0;
```

MIDI is iniatilized and the Flags cleared to zero:

```
MIDI.begin(MIDI_CHANNEL_OMNI);
MIDI.turnThruOn();

for (int x = 0; x < drums; x++) {
  Flag[drums] = 0;
}
}
```

In the main program LOOP the 9 drum touch inputs are read starting with:

```
MIDI.begin(MIDI_CHANNEL_OMNI);
MIDI.turnThruOn();

for (int x = 0; x < drums; x++) {
  Flag[drums] = 0;
}
}
```

In the FOR Loop if the total[n] is greater or equal to the ThresholdOn AND the Flag[n] is LOW then a corresponding MIDI Note On is transmittted, and the Flag[n] is set HIGH:

```
for (n = 0; n < drums; n++) {

  if ((total[n] >= ThresholdOn) && (Flag[n] ==
LOW)) {
    MIDI.sendNoteOn(drumType[n], 100,
MIDIchannel);
    Flag[n] = HIGH;
  }
```

Also in the FOR Loop if the total[n] is less than or equal to the ThresholdOff AND the Flag[n] is HIGH then a corresponding MIDI Note Off is transmittted, and the Flag[n] is cleared to LOW:

```
  if ((total[n] < ThresholdOff) && (Flag[n] ==
HIGH)) {
```

```
    MIDI.sendNoteOff(drumType[n], 100,
MIDIchannel);
    Flag[n] = LOW;
  }
 }
}
```

15.5 *Wiring Layout for 9 Input Drum MIDI Touch Controller*

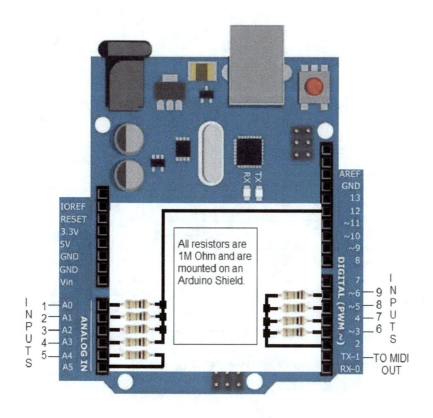

All resistors are 1M Ohm and are mounted on an Arduino Shield.

Figure 35: Wiring Layout for 9 Input MIDI Touch Drum Controller

15.6 Circuit Schematic diagram for 9 Input MIDI Touch Drum Controller

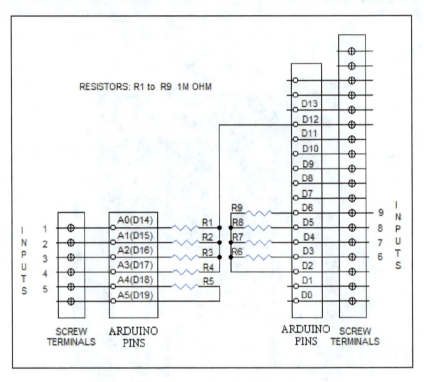

Figure 36: 9 Touch Inputs for 9-Way MIDI Drum Controller

15.7 Circuit Schematic diagram for the 9 Note MIDI Drum Out

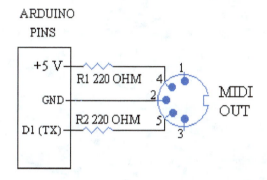

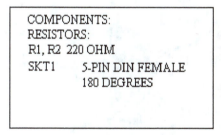

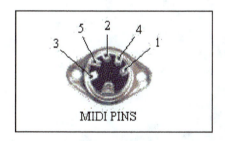

Figure 37: MIDI Out for 9 Input MIDI Touch Drum Controller

15.8 Layout for MIDI Touch Drums

Picture 8: Layout Top of 9 drums

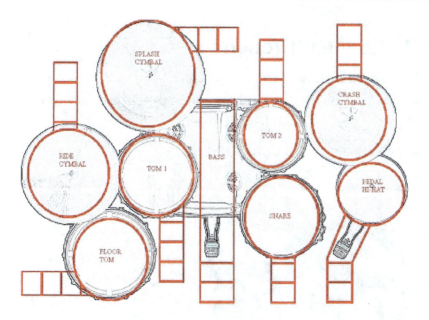

Picture 9: Layout of Drums Back showing Copper Adhesive Tape in Red

A 37 Note MIDI Touch Piano

This design is based on the requirements for a 37 Note touch piano, which allows up to a three octave MIDI instrument to be produced.

Figure 38: MIDI 37 Note Touch Piano Board Connections

16.1 Operation

The 37 note range is from C2 (MIDI Number 36) to C5 (MIDI Number 72). The MIDI Channel is preset to MIDI Channel 1. However other values for the MIDI Channel and the note range can be pre-programmed into the firmware. This unit can work in the standard MIDI Baud rate of 31250.

16.2 Features

The 37 Note MIDI Touch Piano Unit consists of an Arduino Mega 2560 Board, including a suitable pre-programmed microcontroller, the MIDI channel is preset to channel 1, the velocity byte is a fixed value in the firmware, the 37 Note Keyboard ranges from MIDI note 36 (C2) to MIDI note 72 (C5), other MIDI channel and start note values can be pre-programmed in the firmware, a MIDI Activity LED, a MIDI 5-pin DIN output socket and associated series resistors and a USB/MIDI Out socket. Also 37 1M Ohm resistors are needed for the touch inputs.

16.3 Source code for the 37 Note Touch Piano

```
#include <CapacitiveSensor.h>
#include <MIDI.h>

MIDI_CREATE_DEFAULT_INSTANCE();

#define noteCount 37   // number of notes used
in the note range
#define programChangeNum 0   // Piano

CapacitiveSensor   cs_2_54 =
CapacitiveSensor(2, 54);
CapacitiveSensor   cs_2_55 =
CapacitiveSensor(2, 55);
CapacitiveSensor   cs_2_56 =
```

```
CapacitiveSensor(2, 56);
 CapacitiveSensor    cs_2_57 =
CapacitiveSensor(2, 57);
CapacitiveSensor    cs_3_58 =
CapacitiveSensor(3, 58);
CapacitiveSensor    cs_3_59 =
CapacitiveSensor(3, 59);
CapacitiveSensor    cs_3_60 =
CapacitiveSensor(3, 60);
CapacitiveSensor    cs_3_61 =
CapacitiveSensor(3, 61);
CapacitiveSensor    cs_4_22 =
CapacitiveSensor(4, 22);
CapacitiveSensor    cs_4_24 =
CapacitiveSensor(4, 24);
CapacitiveSensor    cs_4_26 =
CapacitiveSensor(4, 26);
CapacitiveSensor    cs_4_28 =
CapacitiveSensor(4, 28);
CapacitiveSensor    cs_5_30 =
CapacitiveSensor(5, 30);
CapacitiveSensor    cs_5_32 =
CapacitiveSensor(5, 32);
CapacitiveSensor    cs_5_34 =
CapacitiveSensor(5, 34);
CapacitiveSensor    cs_5_36 =
CapacitiveSensor(5, 36);
CapacitiveSensor    cs_6_38 =
CapacitiveSensor(6, 38);
CapacitiveSensor    cs_6_40 =
CapacitiveSensor(6, 40);
CapacitiveSensor    cs_6_42 =
CapacitiveSensor(6, 42);
CapacitiveSensor    cs_6_44 =
CapacitiveSensor(6, 44);
CapacitiveSensor    cs_7_46 =
CapacitiveSensor(7, 46);
CapacitiveSensor    cs_7_48 =
CapacitiveSensor(7, 48);
CapacitiveSensor    cs_7_50 =
CapacitiveSensor(7, 50);
CapacitiveSensor    cs_7_52 =
CapacitiveSensor(7, 52);
```

```
CapacitiveSensor   cs_8_23 =
CapacitiveSensor(8, 23);
CapacitiveSensor   cs_8_25 =
CapacitiveSensor(8, 25);
CapacitiveSensor   cs_8_27 =
CapacitiveSensor(8, 27);
CapacitiveSensor   cs_8_29 =
CapacitiveSensor(8, 29);
CapacitiveSensor   cs_9_31 =
CapacitiveSensor(9, 31);
CapacitiveSensor   cs_9_33 =
CapacitiveSensor(9, 33);
CapacitiveSensor   cs_9_35 =
CapacitiveSensor(9, 35);
CapacitiveSensor   cs_9_37 =
CapacitiveSensor(9, 37);
CapacitiveSensor   cs_10_39 =
CapacitiveSensor(10, 39);
CapacitiveSensor   cs_10_41 =
CapacitiveSensor(10, 41);
CapacitiveSensor   cs_10_43 =
CapacitiveSensor(10, 43);
CapacitiveSensor   cs_10_45 =
CapacitiveSensor(10, 45);
CapacitiveSensor   cs_11_47 =
CapacitiveSensor(11, 47);

int note[noteCount] = {
  0, 1, 2, 3, 4, 5, 6, 7, 8, 9, 10, 11, 12, 13,
  14, 15, 16, 17, 18, 19, 20, 21, 22, 23, 24,
25,
  26, 27, 28, 29, 30, 31, 32, 33, 34, 35, 36
};

int ThresholdOn = 500;
int ThresholdOff = 50;
int MIDIchannel = 1;
int startNote = 36; // C2 (MIDI Number 36)
int Flag[noteCount];
long total[noteCount];
int n, x;
//-------------------------------------------------
```

```
void setup()
{
  MIDI.begin(MIDI_CHANNEL_OMNI);
  MIDI.turnThruOn();

  for (x = 0; x < noteCount; x++) {
    Flag[noteCount] = 0;
  }

  MIDI.sendProgramChange(programChangeNum,
MIDIchannel);
}


//-------------------------------------

void loop()
{
  total[0] = cs_2_54.capacitiveSensor(20);
  total[1] = cs_2_55.capacitiveSensor(20);
  total[2] = cs_2_56.capacitiveSensor(20);
  total[3] = cs_2_57.capacitiveSensor(20);
  total[4] = cs_3_58.capacitiveSensor(20);
  total[5] = cs_3_59.capacitiveSensor(20);
  total[6] = cs_3_60.capacitiveSensor(20);
  total[7] = cs_3_61.capacitiveSensor(20);
  total[8] = cs_4_22.capacitiveSensor(20);
  total[9] = cs_4_24.capacitiveSensor(20);
  total[10] = cs_4_26.capacitiveSensor(20);
  total[11] = cs_4_28.capacitiveSensor(20);
  total[12] = cs_5_30.capacitiveSensor(20);
  total[13] = cs_5_32.capacitiveSensor(20);
  total[14] = cs_5_34.capacitiveSensor(20);
  total[15] = cs_5_36.capacitiveSensor(20);
  total[16] = cs_6_38.capacitiveSensor(20);
  total[17] = cs_6_40.capacitiveSensor(20);
  total[18] = cs_6_42.capacitiveSensor(20);
  total[19] = cs_6_44.capacitiveSensor(20);
  total[20] = cs_7_46.capacitiveSensor(20);
  total[21] = cs_7_48.capacitiveSensor(20);
  total[22] = cs_7_50.capacitiveSensor(20);
  total[23] = cs_7_52.capacitiveSensor(20);
  total[24] = cs_8_23.capacitiveSensor(20);
```

```
total[25] = cs_8_25.capacitiveSensor(20);
total[26] = cs_8_27.capacitiveSensor(20);
total[27] = cs_8_29.capacitiveSensor(20);
total[28] = cs_9_31.capacitiveSensor(20);
total[29] = cs_9_33.capacitiveSensor(20);
total[30] = cs_9_35.capacitiveSensor(20);
total[31] = cs_9_37.capacitiveSensor(20);
total[32] = cs_10_39.capacitiveSensor(20);
total[33] = cs_10_41.capacitiveSensor(20);
total[34] = cs_10_43.capacitiveSensor(20);
total[35] = cs_10_45.capacitiveSensor(20);
total[36] = cs_11_47.capacitiveSensor(20);

for (n = 0; n < noteCount; n++) {

    if ((total[n] >= ThresholdOn) && (Flag[n]
== LOW)) {
        MIDI.sendNoteOn(note[n] + startNote, 100,
MIDIchannel);
        Flag[n] = HIGH;
    }

    if ((total[n] < ThresholdOff) && (Flag[n]
== HIGH)) {
        MIDI.sendNoteOff(note[n] + startNote,
100, MIDIchannel);
        Flag[n] = LOW;
    }
  }
}
//----------------------------------
```

Listing 14: Source Code for a 37 Note MIDI Touch Piano

16.4 Explanation of the Source Code

The Capacitive Sensor Library is called using:

```
#include <CapacitiveSensor.h>
```

The source code uses the MIDI Library:

MIDI TOUCH MUSICAL INSTRUMENTS USING THE ARDUINO

```
//https://www.arduino.cc/reference/en/libraries/midi-library/

#include <MIDI.h>
MIDI_CREATE_DEFAULT_INSTANCE();
```

MIDI commands are initialized by:

```
MIDI.begin(MIDI_CHANNEL_OMNI);
```

The touch switches are initialized with the starting line:

```
CapacitiveSensor   cs_2_54 = CapacitiveSensor(2, 54);
```

The Variables and Constants are initialized with:

```
int note[noteCount] = {
  0, 1, 2, 3, 4, 5, 6, 7, 8, 9, 10, 11, 12, 13,
  14, 15, 16, 17, 18, 19, 20, 21, 22, 23, 24, 25,
  26, 27, 28, 29, 30, 31, 32, 33, 34, 35, 36
};

int ThresholdOn = 500;
int ThresholdOff = 50;
int MIDIchannel = 1;
int startNote = 36; // C2 (MIDI Number 36)
int Flag[noteCount];
long total[noteCount];
int n, x;
```

The Setup routine initialises MIDI, clears the Flags and sensa a MIDI Program Change command:

```
MIDI.begin(MIDI_CHANNEL_OMNI);
MIDI.turnThruOn();

for (x = 0; x < noteCount; x++) {
  Flag[noteCount] = 0;
}
```

```
MIDI.sendProgramChange(programChangeNum,
MIDIchannel);
```

The main Loop routine reads the 37 switches starting with:

```
total[0] = cs_2_54.capacitiveSensor(20);
```

In the FOR Loop if the total[n] is greater or equal to the ThresholdOn AND the Flag[n] is LOW then a corresponding MIDI Note On is transmittted, and the Flag[n] is set HIGH:

```
if ((total[n] >= ThresholdOn) && (Flag[n] ==
LOW)) {
    MIDI.sendNoteOn(note[n] + startNote, 100,
MIDIchannel); // Send a Note (pitch, velocity 100
on MIDI channel )
    Flag[n] = HIGH;
```

Also in the FOR Loop if the total[n] is less than or equal to the ThresholdOff AND the Flag[n] is HIGH then a corresponding MIDI Note Off is transmittted, and the Flag[n] is cleared to LOW:

```
if ((total[n] < ThresholdOff) && (Flag[n] ==
HIGH)) {
    MIDI.sendNoteOff(note[n] + startNote, 100,
MIDIchannel);
    Flag[n] = LOW;
}
```

16.5 *Circuit schematic diagram for the 37 Note MIDI Touch Piano Encoder*

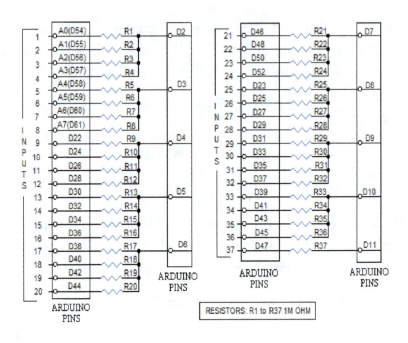

Figure 39: Circuit Schematic for a 37 Note MIDI Touch Piano Instrument

16.6 MIDI Out Circuit Schematic diagram for the 37 Note Piano

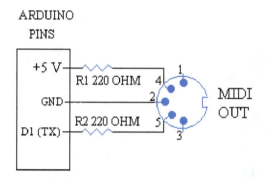

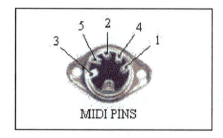

MIDI PINS

Figure 40: MIDI Out for a 37 Note MIDI Touch Piano

16.7 Layout for a 37 Note MIDI Touch Piano

Picture 10: Layout of 37 Note MIDI Touch Piano

16.8 Rear Wiring and Resistors for a 37 Note MIDI Touch Piano

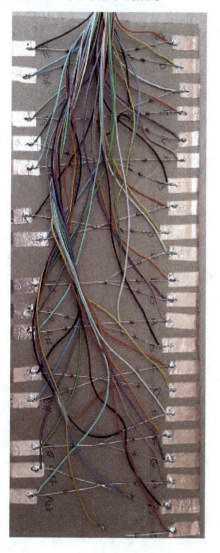

Picture 11: Rear Wiring and Resistors for 37 Note MIDI Touch Piano

A Brief Introduction to Percussion Instruments

Percussion instruments include any instrument that makes a sound when it is hit, shaken, or scraped. Some percussion instruments are tuned and can sound different notes, for example like the xylophone, vibraphone, marimba or glockenspiel, and some are untuned with no definite pitch, for example drums, cymbals or castanets.

17.1 An Introduction to Tuned Percussion Instruments

The label tuned percussion is a an accurate name for this family of musical instruments. The percussion instrument part comes from the fact that the player hits them and the tuned part comes from the fact that each bar of the instrument has a different pitch.

Unlike most of the other players in the orchestra, a percussionist will usually play many different instruments in one piece of music. The most common percussion instruments in the orchestra include the timpani, xylophone, cymbals, triangle, snare drum, bass drum, tambourine, maracas, gongs, chimes and celesta.

17.2 Tuned percussion instruments pitch note ranges

Tuned percussion instruments like a vibraphone, xylophone, marimba or glockenspiel can have different pitch note ranges.

Vibraphones

The Vibraphone can have a pitch range of up to four octaves, from C3 (MIDI Note 48) up to C7 (MIDI Note 96). However, instruments with a range of three octaves are much more common, from F3 (MIDI Note 53) up to F6 (MIDI Note 89). The vibraphone is generally a non-transposing instrument, written at concert pitch, and it is notated sounding in the treble clef.

Xylophones

A xylophone pitch range is commonly three and a half octaves and goes from F3 (MIDI Note 53) up to C7 (MIDI Note 96), usually sounding 1 octave higher than written. Commercial sizes can have as few as three octaves and as many as five octaves.

Marimbas

There is no standard pitch range for the marimba, but the most common ranges are four, four and a third, four and a half and five octave sizes.

A four octave marimba has the range from C3 (MIDI Note 48) up to C7 (MIDI Note 96).

A four and a third octave marimba has the range from A2 (MIDI Note 45) up to C7 (MIDI Note 96).

A four and a half octave marimba has the range from F2 (MIDI Note 41) up to C7 (MIDI Note 96).

A 5 octave marimba has the range of C2 (MIDI Note 36) up to C7 (MIDI Note 96).

Glockenspiel

The pitch range is two and a half or, occasionally, three octaves, the highest note is normally the third C above middle C, which is C7 (MIDI Note 96).

The glockenspiel is often a transposing instrument and sounds two octaves above the written pitch, although this is sometimes remedied by using an octave clef.

A Two and a Half Octave MIDI Touch Glockenspiel

The Glockenspiel pitch range is two and a half or, occasionally, three octaves, the highest note is normally the third C above middle C, which is C7 (MIDI Note 96). The glockenspiel is often a transposing instrument and sounds two octaves above the written pitch.

18.1 Operation

This design is for a two and a half octave 30 Note Glockenspiel with the range from G4 (MIDI Note 67) up to C7 (MIDI Note 96). The MIDI Channel is preset to MIDI Channel 1. However other values for the MIDI Channel and the note range can be pre-programmed into the firmware. This unit can work in the standard MIDI Baud rate of 31250.

18.2 Features

The two and a half octave 30 Note MIDI Glockenspiel Unit consists of an Arduino Mega 2560 Board, including a suitable pre-programmed microcontroller, the MIDI channel is preset to channel 1, the velocity byte is a fixed value in the firmware, the 30 Note Keyboard ranges from MIDI from G4 (MIDI Note 67) up to C7 (MIDI Note 96), other MIDI channel and start note values can be pre-programmed, if required, MIDI Activity LED, a MIDI 5-pin DIN output socket and associated series resistors and a USB/MIDI Out socket. Also 30 1M Ohm resistors are needed for the touch inputs.

18.3 Software Features

The software includes the addition of a delay/decay time loop. Since the sound of most Tuned Percussion instruments have a relatively long decay time, there is provision in the software to allow this element to be adjusted in the firmware. It is designed to allow notes to be played rapidly, if required, but also to allow the sound to decay slowly.

18.4 Source code for the Two and a Half Octave 30 Note MIDI Touch Glockenspiel

```
/*
 General MIDI Program Change percussion:
 0x08  8 Celesta
 0x09   9 Glockenspiel
 0x0A  10  Music box
 0x0B  11  Vibraphone
 0x0C  12  Marimba
 0x0D  13  Xylophone
 0x0E  14  Tubular bell
 0x0F  15  Dulcimer
*/

#include <CapacitiveSensor.h>
#include <MIDI.h>

MIDI_CREATE_DEFAULT_INSTANCE();

#define noteCount 30   // number of notes used
in the note range
#define programChangeNum 9  // Glockenspiel

CapacitiveSensor    cs_2_54 =
CapacitiveSensor(2, 54);
CapacitiveSensor    cs_2_55 =
CapacitiveSensor(2, 55);
CapacitiveSensor    cs_2_56 =
CapacitiveSensor(2, 56);
```

```
CapacitiveSensor   cs_2_57 =
CapacitiveSensor(2, 57);
CapacitiveSensor   cs_3_58 =
CapacitiveSensor(3, 58);
CapacitiveSensor   cs_3_59 =
CapacitiveSensor(3, 59);
CapacitiveSensor   cs_3_60 =
CapacitiveSensor(3, 60);
CapacitiveSensor   cs_3_61 =
CapacitiveSensor(3, 61);
CapacitiveSensor   cs_4_22 =
CapacitiveSensor(4, 22);
CapacitiveSensor   cs_4_24 =
CapacitiveSensor(4, 24);
CapacitiveSensor   cs_4_26 =
CapacitiveSensor(4, 26);
CapacitiveSensor   cs_4_28 =
CapacitiveSensor(4, 28);
CapacitiveSensor   cs_5_30 =
CapacitiveSensor(5, 30);
CapacitiveSensor   cs_5_32 =
CapacitiveSensor(5, 32);
CapacitiveSensor   cs_5_34 =
CapacitiveSensor(5, 34);
CapacitiveSensor   cs_5_36 =
CapacitiveSensor(5, 36);
CapacitiveSensor   cs_6_38 =
CapacitiveSensor(6, 38);
CapacitiveSensor   cs_6_40 =
CapacitiveSensor(6, 40);
CapacitiveSensor   cs_6_42 =
CapacitiveSensor(6, 42);
CapacitiveSensor   cs_6_44 =
CapacitiveSensor(6, 44);
CapacitiveSensor   cs_7_46 =
CapacitiveSensor(7, 46);
CapacitiveSensor   cs_7_48 =
CapacitiveSensor(7, 48);
CapacitiveSensor   cs_7_50 =
CapacitiveSensor(7, 50);
CapacitiveSensor   cs_7_52 =
CapacitiveSensor(7, 52);
CapacitiveSensor   cs_8_23 =
```

```
CapacitiveSensor(8, 23);
CapacitiveSensor    cs_8_25 =
CapacitiveSensor(8, 25);
CapacitiveSensor    cs_8_27 =
CapacitiveSensor(8, 27);
CapacitiveSensor    cs_8_29 =
CapacitiveSensor(8, 29);
CapacitiveSensor    cs_9_31 =
CapacitiveSensor(9, 31);
CapacitiveSensor    cs_9_33 =
CapacitiveSensor(9, 33);

int note[noteCount] = {
  0, 1, 2, 3, 4, 5, 6, 7, 8, 9, 10, 11, 12, 13,
  14, 15, 16, 17, 18, 19, 20, 21, 22, 23, 24,
25,
  26, 27, 28, 29
};

int ThresholdOn = 500;
int ThresholdOff = 50;
int MIDIchannel = 1;
int startNote = 67; // Note G4
int Flag[noteCount];
int decayFlag[noteCount];
long total[noteCount];
int n, x;
unsigned long noteStartTime[noteCount];
unsigned long decayTime = 2000; // 2000 ms

//------------------------------------------------
--

void setup()
{
  MIDI.begin(MIDI_CHANNEL_OMNI);
  MIDI.turnThruOn();

  for (x = 0; x < noteCount; x++) {
    Flag[noteCount] = 0;
    decayFlag[noteCount] = 0;
  }
```

```
  MIDI.sendProgramChange(programChangeNum,
MIDIchannel);
}


//--------------------------------------

void loop()
{

  total[0] = cs_2_54.capacitiveSensor(20);
  total[1] = cs_2_55.capacitiveSensor(20);
  total[2] = cs_2_56.capacitiveSensor(20);
  total[3] = cs_2_57.capacitiveSensor(20);
  total[4] = cs_3_58.capacitiveSensor(20);
  total[5] = cs_3_59.capacitiveSensor(20);
  total[6] = cs_3_60.capacitiveSensor(20);
  total[7] = cs_3_61.capacitiveSensor(20);
  total[8] = cs_4_22.capacitiveSensor(20);
  total[9] = cs_4_24.capacitiveSensor(20);
  total[10] = cs_4_26.capacitiveSensor(20);
  total[11] = cs_4_28.capacitiveSensor(20);
  total[12] = cs_5_30.capacitiveSensor(20);
  total[13] = cs_5_32.capacitiveSensor(20);
  total[14] = cs_5_34.capacitiveSensor(20);
  total[15] = cs_5_36.capacitiveSensor(20);
  total[16] = cs_6_38.capacitiveSensor(20);
  total[17] = cs_6_40.capacitiveSensor(20);
  total[18] = cs_6_42.capacitiveSensor(20);
  total[19] = cs_6_44.capacitiveSensor(20);
  total[20] = cs_7_46.capacitiveSensor(20);
  total[21] = cs_7_48.capacitiveSensor(20);
  total[22] = cs_7_50.capacitiveSensor(20);
  total[23] = cs_7_52.capacitiveSensor(20);
  total[24] = cs_8_23.capacitiveSensor(20);
  total[25] = cs_8_25.capacitiveSensor(20);
  total[26] = cs_8_27.capacitiveSensor(20);
  total[27] = cs_8_29.capacitiveSensor(20);
  total[28] = cs_9_31.capacitiveSensor(20);
  total[29] = cs_9_33.capacitiveSensor(20);

  for (n = 0; n < noteCount; n++) {

    if ((total[n] >= ThresholdOn) && (Flag[n]
```

```
== LOW)) {
     MIDI.sendNoteOn(note[n] + startNote, 100,
MIDIchannel); // Send a Note (pitch, velocity
100 on MIDI channel )
     noteStartTime[n] = millis();
     Flag[n] = HIGH;
     decayFlag[n] = HIGH;
   }

   if ((total[n] < ThresholdOff) && (Flag[n]
== HIGH)) {
     Flag[n] = LOW;
   }

   if (( millis() - noteStartTime[n] >=
decayTime) && (decayFlag[n] == HIGH)) {
     MIDI.sendNoteOff(note[n] + startNote,
100, MIDIchannel);
     Flag[n] = LOW;
     decayFlag[n] = LOW;
   }
  }
}
//----------------------------------
```

Listing 15: Source Code for a Two and a Half Octave Touch Glockenspiel

18.5 Explanation of the Source Code

The Capacitive Sensor Library is called using:

```
#include <CapacitiveSensor.h>
```

The source code uses the MIDI Library:

```
//https://www.arduino.cc/reference/en/libraries/m
idi-library/
```

```
#include <MIDI.h>
```

```
MIDI_CREATE_DEFAULT_INSTANCE();
```

MIDI commands are initialized by:

```
MIDI.begin(MIDI_CHANNEL_OMNI);
```

The noteCount is set to 30 and the Program Change number is set to 9 which is the Glochenspiel:

```
#define noteCount 30   // number of notes used in
the note range
#define programChangeNum 9   // Glockenspiel
```

The touch switches are initialized with the starting line:

```
CapacitiveSensor   cs_2_54 = CapacitiveSensor(2,
54);
```

The Variables and Constants are initialized with:

```
int note[noteCount] = {
   0, 1, 2, 3, 4, 5, 6, 7, 8, 9, 10, 11, 12, 13,
   14, 15, 16, 17, 18, 19, 20, 21, 22, 23, 24, 25,
   26, 27, 28, 29
};

int ThresholdOn = 500;
int ThresholdOff = 50;
int MIDIchannel = 1;
int startNote = 67; // Note G4
int Flag[noteCount];
int decayFlag[noteCount];
long total[noteCount];
int n, x;
unsigned long noteStartTime[noteCount];
unsigned long decayTime = 2000; // 2000 ms
```

The Setup routine initialises MIDI, clears the Flags and sends a MIDI Program Change command:

```
MIDI.begin(MIDI_CHANNEL_OMNI);
MIDI.turnThruOn();

for (x = 0; x < noteCount; x++) {
  Flag[noteCount] = 0;
}

MIDI.sendProgramChange(programChangeNum,
MIDIchannel);
```

The main Loop routine reads the 30 switches starting with:

```
total[0] = cs_2_54.capacitiveSensor(20);
```

In the FOR Loop if the total[n] is greater or equal to the ThresholdOn AND the Flag[n] is LOW then a corresponding MIDI Note On is transmittted, the present time millis() is stored in noteStartTime[n], the Flag[n] is set HIGH and the decayFlag[n] is set HIGH:

```
for (n = 0; n < noteCount; n++) {

   if ((total[n] >= ThresholdOn) && (Flag[n] ==
LOW)) {
      MIDI.sendNoteOn(note[n] + startNote, 100,
MIDIchannel); // Send a Note (pitch, velocity 100
on MIDI channel )
      noteStartTime[n] = millis();
      Flag[n] = HIGH;
      decayFlag[n] = HIGH;
   }
```

Also in the FOR Loop if the total[n] is less than the ThresholdOff AND the Flag[n] is HIGH then a corresponding MIDI Note Off is transmittted, and the Flag[n] is set LOW:

```
   if ((total[n] < ThresholdOff) && (Flag[n] ==
HIGH)) {
      Flag[n] = LOW;
   }
```

```
    if (( millis() - noteStartTime[n] >=
decayTime) && (decayFlag[n] == HIGH)) {
      MIDI.sendNoteOff(note[n] + startNote, 100,
MIDIchannel);
      Flag[n] = LOW;
      decayFlag[n] = LOW;
    }
  }
}
```

18.6 Circuit Schematic Diagram for the Two and a Half 30 Note MIDI Touch Glockenspiel

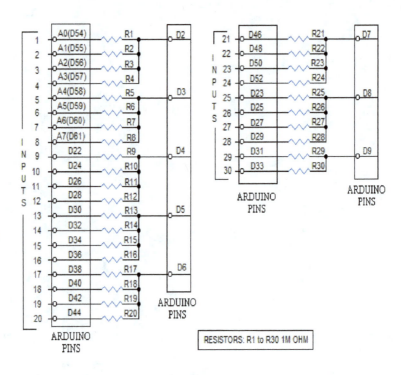

Figure 41: Circuit Schematic for 30 Note MIDI Touch Glockenspiel Inputs

18.7 MIDI Out Circuit Schematic diagram for the 30 Note Glockenspiel

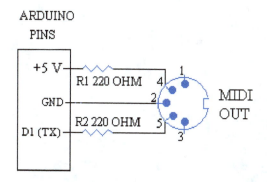

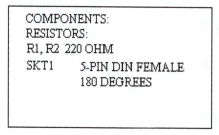

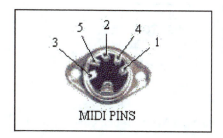

MIDI PINS

Figure 42: MIDI Out for the 30 Note Glockenspiel

18.8 The MIDI Out Wiring for Two and a Half Octave Touch Glockenspiel Encoder

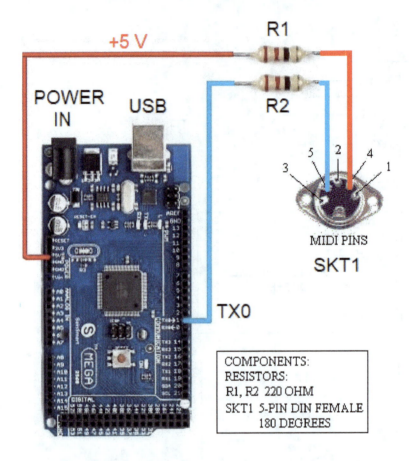

Figure 43: MIDI Out Wiring for 30 Note MIDI Touch Glockenspiel

A 3 Octave MIDI Touch Vibraphone

Vibraphones can have a pitch range of up to four octaves, from C3 (MIDI Note 48) up to C7 (MIDI Note 96). However, instruments with a range of three octaves are much more common, from F3 (MIDI Note 53) up to F6 (MIDI Note 89). The vibraphone is generally a non-transposing instrument, written at concert pitch, and it is notated sounding in the treble clef.

This design is for a 3 octave 37 Note MIDI Touch Vibraphone with the note range from F3 (MIDI Note 53) up to F6 (MIDI Note 89).

Figure 44: Arduino Mega 2560 for MIDI Touch Vibraphone

19.1 Features

The 37 Note MIDI Touch Vibraphone Encoder Unit consists of an Arduino Mega 2560 Board, including a suitable pre-programmed microcontroller, the MIDI channel is preset to channel 1, the velocity byte is a fixed value in the firmware, the 37 Note MIDI Touch Vibraphone Encoder ranges from F3 (MIDI Note 53) up to F6 (MIDI Note 89), a MIDI Activity LED, a MIDI 5-pin DIN output socket and associated series resistors and a USB/MIDI Out socket. Also 37 1M Ohm resistors are needed for the touch inputs.

19.2 Software Features

The software is similar to the MIDI Touch Piano software but has a major difference. It has the addition of a delay/decay time loop. Since the sound of most Tuned Percussion instruments have a relatively long decay time. The design includes an adjustable Note Off delay in the software. This allows the note to continue sounding even after the mallet/finger that has hit/touched it has been removed. It is designed to allow notes to be played rapidly, if required, but also to allow the sound to decay slowly.

19.3 Source code for the 3 Octave MIDI Touch Vibraphone

```
/*
General MIDI Program Change percussion:
0x08 8 Celesta
0x09  9 Glockenspiel
0x0A  10  Music box
0x0B  11  Vibraphone
0x0C  12  Marimba
0x0D  13  Xylophone
0x0E  14  Tubular bell
0x0F  15  Dulcimer
*/
```

```cpp
#include <CapacitiveSensor.h>
#include <MIDI.h>

MIDI_CREATE_DEFAULT_INSTANCE();

#define noteCount 37  // number of notes used
in the note range
#define programChangeNum 11  // Vibraphone

CapacitiveSensor   cs_2_54 =
CapacitiveSensor(2, 54);
CapacitiveSensor   cs_2_55 =
CapacitiveSensor(2, 55);
CapacitiveSensor   cs_2_56 =
CapacitiveSensor(2, 56);
CapacitiveSensor   cs_2_57 =
CapacitiveSensor(2, 57);
CapacitiveSensor   cs_3_58 =
CapacitiveSensor(3, 58);
CapacitiveSensor   cs_3_59 =
CapacitiveSensor(3, 59);
CapacitiveSensor   cs_3_60 =
CapacitiveSensor(3, 60);
CapacitiveSensor   cs_3_61 =
CapacitiveSensor(3, 61);
CapacitiveSensor   cs_4_22 =
CapacitiveSensor(4, 22);
CapacitiveSensor   cs_4_24 =
CapacitiveSensor(4, 24);
CapacitiveSensor   cs_4_26 =
CapacitiveSensor(4, 26);
CapacitiveSensor   cs_4_28 =
CapacitiveSensor(4, 28);
CapacitiveSensor   cs_5_30 =
CapacitiveSensor(5, 30);
CapacitiveSensor   cs_5_32 =
CapacitiveSensor(5, 32);
CapacitiveSensor   cs_5_34 =
CapacitiveSensor(5, 34);
CapacitiveSensor   cs_5_36 =
CapacitiveSensor(5, 36);
CapacitiveSensor   cs_6_38 =
```

```
CapacitiveSensor(6, 38);
CapacitiveSensor   cs_6_40 =
CapacitiveSensor(6, 40);
CapacitiveSensor   cs_6_42 =
CapacitiveSensor(6, 42);
CapacitiveSensor   cs_6_44 =
CapacitiveSensor(6, 44);
CapacitiveSensor   cs_7_46 =
CapacitiveSensor(7, 46);
CapacitiveSensor   cs_7_48 =
CapacitiveSensor(7, 48);
CapacitiveSensor   cs_7_50 =
CapacitiveSensor(7, 50);
CapacitiveSensor   cs_7_52 =
CapacitiveSensor(7, 52);
CapacitiveSensor   cs_8_23 =
CapacitiveSensor(8, 23);
CapacitiveSensor   cs_8_25 =
CapacitiveSensor(8, 25);
CapacitiveSensor   cs_8_27 =
CapacitiveSensor(8, 27);
CapacitiveSensor   cs_8_29 =
CapacitiveSensor(8, 29);
CapacitiveSensor   cs_9_31 =
CapacitiveSensor(9, 31);
CapacitiveSensor   cs_9_33 =
CapacitiveSensor(9, 33);
CapacitiveSensor   cs_9_35 =
CapacitiveSensor(9, 35);
CapacitiveSensor   cs_9_37 =
CapacitiveSensor(9, 37);
CapacitiveSensor   cs_10_39 =
CapacitiveSensor(10, 39);
CapacitiveSensor   cs_10_41 =
CapacitiveSensor(10, 41);
CapacitiveSensor   cs_10_43 =
CapacitiveSensor(10, 43);
CapacitiveSensor   cs_10_45 =
CapacitiveSensor(10, 45);
CapacitiveSensor   cs_11_47 =
CapacitiveSensor(11, 47);

int note[noteCount] = {
```

```
  0, 1, 2, 3, 4, 5, 6, 7, 8, 9, 10, 11, 12, 13,
   14, 15, 16, 17, 18, 19, 20, 21, 22, 23, 24,
25, 26, 27, 28, 29, 30, 31, 32, 33, 34, 35, 36
};

int ThresholdOn = 500;
int ThresholdOff = 50;
int MIDIchannel = 1;
int startNote = 53; // Note F3
int Flag[noteCount];
int decayFlag[noteCount];
long total[noteCount];
int n, x;
unsigned long noteStartTime[noteCount];
unsigned long decayTime = 2000; // 2000 ms

//---------------------------------------------

void setup()
{
  MIDI.begin(MIDI_CHANNEL_OMNI);
  MIDI.turnThruOn();

  for (x = 0; x < noteCount; x++) {
    Flag[noteCount] = 0;
    decayFlag[noteCount] = 0;
  }

  MIDI.sendProgramChange(programChangeNum,
MIDIchannel);
}

//------------------------------------

void loop()
{

  total[0] = cs_2_54.capacitiveSensor(20);
  total[1] = cs_2_55.capacitiveSensor(20);
  total[2] = cs_2_56.capacitiveSensor(20);
  total[3] = cs_2_57.capacitiveSensor(20);
  total[4] = cs_3_58.capacitiveSensor(20);
  total[5] = cs_3_59.capacitiveSensor(20);
```

```
  total[6] = cs_3_60.capacitiveSensor(20);
  total[7] = cs_3_61.capacitiveSensor(20);
  total[8] = cs_4_22.capacitiveSensor(20);
  total[9] = cs_4_24.capacitiveSensor(20);
  total[10] = cs_4_26.capacitiveSensor(20);
  total[11] = cs_4_28.capacitiveSensor(20);
  total[12] = cs_5_30.capacitiveSensor(20);
  total[13] = cs_5_32.capacitiveSensor(20);
  total[14] = cs_5_34.capacitiveSensor(20);
  total[15] = cs_5_36.capacitiveSensor(20);
  total[16] = cs_6_38.capacitiveSensor(20);
  total[17] = cs_6_40.capacitiveSensor(20);
  total[18] = cs_6_42.capacitiveSensor(20);
  total[19] = cs_6_44.capacitiveSensor(20);
  total[20] = cs_7_46.capacitiveSensor(20);
  total[21] = cs_7_48.capacitiveSensor(20);
  total[22] = cs_7_50.capacitiveSensor(20);
  total[23] = cs_7_52.capacitiveSensor(20);
  total[24] = cs_8_23.capacitiveSensor(20);
  total[25] = cs_8_25.capacitiveSensor(20);
  total[26] = cs_8_27.capacitiveSensor(20);
  total[27] = cs_8_29.capacitiveSensor(20);
  total[28] = cs_9_31.capacitiveSensor(20);
  total[29] = cs_9_33.capacitiveSensor(20);
  total[30] = cs_9_35.capacitiveSensor(20);
  total[31] = cs_9_37.capacitiveSensor(20);
  total[32] = cs_10_39.capacitiveSensor(20);
  total[33] = cs_10_41.capacitiveSensor(20);
  total[34] = cs_10_43.capacitiveSensor(20);
  total[35] = cs_10_45.capacitiveSensor(20);
  total[36] = cs_11_47.capacitiveSensor(20);


  for (n = 0; n < noteCount; n++) {

    if ((total[n] >= ThresholdOn) && (Flag[n]
== LOW)) {
      MIDI.sendNoteOn(note[n] + startNote, 100,
MIDIchannel); // Send a Note (pitch, velocity
100 on MIDI channel )
      noteStartTime[n] = millis();
      Flag[n] = HIGH;
      decayFlag[n] = HIGH;
```

```
    }

    if ((total[n] < ThresholdOff) && (Flag[n]
== HIGH)) {
        Flag[n] = LOW;
    }

    if (( millis() - noteStartTime[n] >=
decayTime) && (decayFlag[n] == HIGH)) {
        MIDI.sendNoteOff(note[n] + startNote,
100, MIDIchannel);
        Flag[n] = LOW;
        decayFlag[n] = LOW;
    }
  }
}
//--------------------------------
```

Listing 16: Source Code for a 3 Octave MIDI Touch Vibraphone

19.4 Explanation of the Source Code

The Capacitive Sensor Library is called using:

```
#include <CapacitiveSensor.h>
```

The source code uses the MIDI Library:

```
//https://www.arduino.cc/reference/en/libraries/m
idi-library/
```

```
#include <MIDI.h>
MIDI_CREATE_DEFAULT_INSTANCE();
```

MIDI commands are initialized by:

```
  MIDI.begin(MIDI_CHANNEL_OMNI);
```

The noteCount is set to 37 and the Program Change number is set to 11 which is the Vibraphone:

```
#define noteCount 37  // number of notes used in
the note range
#define programChangeNum 11  // Vibraphone
```

The touch switches are initialized with the starting line:

```
CapacitiveSensor    cs_2_54 = CapacitiveSensor(2,
54);
```

The Variables and Constants are initialized with:

```
int note[noteCount] = {
  0, 1, 2, 3, 4, 5, 6, 7, 8, 9, 10, 11, 12, 13,
  14, 15, 16, 17, 18, 19, 20, 21, 22, 23, 24, 25,
26, 27, 28, 29, 30, 31, 32, 33, 34, 35, 36
};

int ThresholdOn = 500;
int ThresholdOff = 50;
int MIDIchannel = 1;
int startNote = 53; // Note F3
int Flag[noteCount];
int decayFlag[noteCount];
long total[noteCount];
int n, x;
unsigned long noteStartTime[noteCount];
unsigned long decayTime = 2000; // 2000 ms
```

The Setup routine initialises MIDI, clears the Flags and sends a MIDI Program Change command:

```
  MIDI.begin(MIDI_CHANNEL_OMNI);
  MIDI.turnThruOn();

  for (x = 0; x < noteCount; x++) {
    Flag[noteCount] = 0;
  }

  MIDI.sendProgramChange(programChangeNum,
MIDIchannel);
```

The main Loop routine reads the 37 switches starting with:

```
total[0] = cs_2_54.capacitiveSensor(20);
```

In the FOR Loop if the total[n] is greater or equal to the ThresholdOn AND the Flag[n] is LOW then a corresponding MIDI Note On is transmittted, the present time millis() is stored in noteStartTime[n], the Flag[n] is set HIGH and the decayFlag[n] is set HIGH:

```
for (n = 0; n < noteCount; n++) {

    if ((total[n] >= ThresholdOn) && (Flag[n] ==
LOW)) {
        MIDI.sendNoteOn(note[n] + startNote, 100,
MIDIchannel); // Send a Note (pitch, velocity 100
on MIDI channel )
        noteStartTime[n] = millis();
        Flag[n] = HIGH;
        decayFlag[n] = HIGH;
    }
```

Also in the FOR Loop if the total[n] is less than the ThresholdOff AND the Flag[n] is HIGH then a corresponding MIDI Note Off is transmittted, and the Flag[n] is set LOW:

```
    if ((total[n] < ThresholdOff) && (Flag[n] ==
HIGH)) {
        Flag[n] = LOW;
    }

    if (( millis() - noteStartTime[n] >=
decayTime) && (decayFlag[n] == HIGH)) {
        MIDI.sendNoteOff(note[n] + startNote, 100,
MIDIchannel);
        Flag[n] = LOW;
        decayFlag[n] = LOW;
    }
  }
}
```

19.5 Circuit schematic diagram for the 3 Octave MIDI Touch Vibraphone Encoder

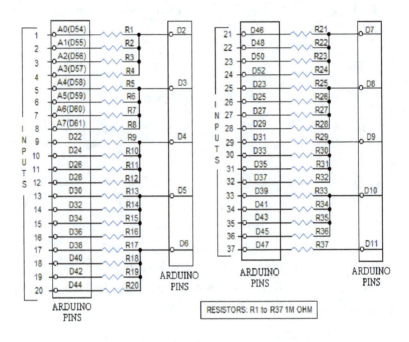

Figure 45: Circuit Schematic for a 3 Octave MIDI Touch Vibraphone

19.6 MIDI Out Circuit Schematic for the 3 Octave Vibraphone

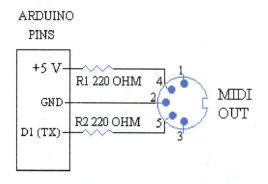

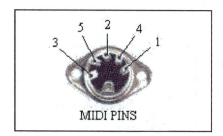

Figure 46: MIDI Out for the 3 Octave Vibraphone

19.7 The MIDI Out Wiring for 3 Octave Touch Vibraphone Encoder

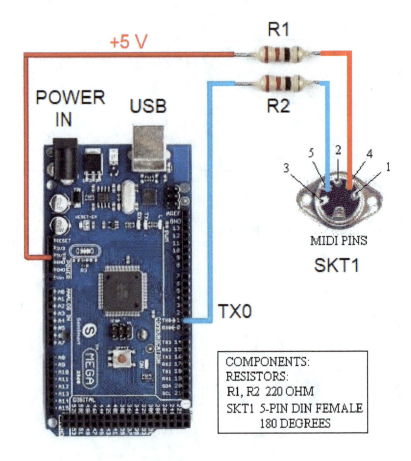

Figure 47: MIDI Out Wiring for 3 Octave Touch Vibraphone Encoder

A 5 Octave MIDI Touch Marimba

This design is based on the requirements for up to a 73 Note tuned percussion instrument like a vibraphone, xylophone, marimba or glockenspiel. So this design allows up to a six octave MIDI mallet percussion family instrument to be produced. This particular design is for a 5 Octave MIDI Touch Marimba.

The design utilizes a combination of two 37 Note Arduino Mega 2560 boards, with the MIDI Output of board 1 connected to the MIDI Input of board 2.

20.1 Features

The 5 Octave MIDI Touch Marimba Encoder Unit consists of the combination of two Arduino Mega 2560 Boards, including suitable pre-programmed microcontrollers, the MIDI channel is preset to channel 1, the velocity byte is a fixed value in the firmware, the 5 Octave MIDI Touch Marimba Encoder ranges from C2 (MIDI Note 36) up to C7 (MIDI Note 96), a MIDI Activity LED, a MIDI 5-pin DIN output socket and associated series resistors and a USB/MIDI Out socket. Also 61 1M Ohm resistors are needed for the touch inputs.

20.2 Wiring Features

The design uses the combination of two Arduino Mega boards, with Board 1 having 37 touch inputs and Board 2 having 24 notes to give a total of 61 notes to produce 5 octaves. So Board 1 has the 37 note range from C2 (MIDI Note 36) up to C5 (MIDI Note 72) and Board 2 has 24 touch inputs from C#5 (MIDI Note 73) up to C7 (MIDI Note 96).

20.3 Software Features

The software has the addition of a delay/decay time loop. Since the sound of most Tuned Percussion instruments have a relatively long decay time. The design includes an adjustable Note Off delay in the software. This allows the note to continue sounding even after the mallet/finger that has hit/touched it has been removed. It is designed to allow notes to be played rapidly, if required, but also to allow the sound to decay slowly.

20.4 Source code for the 5 Octave MIDI Touch Marimba Encoder 1

```
/*
General MIDI Program Change percussion:
0x08  8 Celesta
0x09  9 Glockenspiel
0x0A  10  Music box
0x0B  11  Vibraphone
0x0C  12  Marimba
0x0D  13  Xylophone
0x0E  14  Tubular bell
0x0F  15  Dulcimer
*/

#include <CapacitiveSensor.h>
#include <MIDI.h>

MIDI_CREATE_DEFAULT_INSTANCE();

#define noteCount 37  // number of notes used
in the note range
#define programChangeNum 12  // Marimba

CapacitiveSensor    cs_2_54 =
CapacitiveSensor(2, 54);
CapacitiveSensor    cs_2_55 =
CapacitiveSensor(2, 55);
CapacitiveSensor    cs_2_56 =
```

```
CapacitiveSensor(2, 56);
CapacitiveSensor    cs_2_57 =
CapacitiveSensor(2, 57);
CapacitiveSensor    cs_3_58 =
CapacitiveSensor(3, 58);
CapacitiveSensor    cs_3_59 =
CapacitiveSensor(3, 59);
CapacitiveSensor    cs_3_60 =
CapacitiveSensor(3, 60);
CapacitiveSensor    cs_3_61 =
CapacitiveSensor(3, 61);
CapacitiveSensor    cs_4_22 =
CapacitiveSensor(4, 22);
CapacitiveSensor    cs_4_24 =
CapacitiveSensor(4, 24);
CapacitiveSensor    cs_4_26 =
CapacitiveSensor(4, 26);
CapacitiveSensor    cs_4_28 =
CapacitiveSensor(4, 28);
CapacitiveSensor    cs_5_30 =
CapacitiveSensor(5, 30);
CapacitiveSensor    cs_5_32 =
CapacitiveSensor(5, 32);
CapacitiveSensor    cs_5_34 =
CapacitiveSensor(5, 34);
CapacitiveSensor    cs_5_36 =
CapacitiveSensor(5, 36);
CapacitiveSensor    cs_6_38 =
CapacitiveSensor(6, 38);
CapacitiveSensor    cs_6_40 =
CapacitiveSensor(6, 40);
CapacitiveSensor    cs_6_42 =
CapacitiveSensor(6, 42);
CapacitiveSensor    cs_6_44 =
CapacitiveSensor(6, 44);
CapacitiveSensor    cs_7_46 =
CapacitiveSensor(7, 46);
CapacitiveSensor    cs_7_48 =
CapacitiveSensor(7, 48);
CapacitiveSensor    cs_7_50 =
CapacitiveSensor(7, 50);
CapacitiveSensor    cs_7_52 =
CapacitiveSensor(7, 52);
```

```
CapacitiveSensor   cs_8_23 =
CapacitiveSensor(8, 23);
CapacitiveSensor   cs_8_25 =
CapacitiveSensor(8, 25);
CapacitiveSensor   cs_8_27 =
CapacitiveSensor(8, 27);
CapacitiveSensor   cs_8_29 =
CapacitiveSensor(8, 29);
CapacitiveSensor   cs_9_31 =
CapacitiveSensor(9, 31);
CapacitiveSensor   cs_9_33 =
CapacitiveSensor(9, 33);
CapacitiveSensor   cs_9_35 =
CapacitiveSensor(9, 35);
CapacitiveSensor   cs_9_37 =
CapacitiveSensor(9, 37);
CapacitiveSensor   cs_10_39 =
CapacitiveSensor(10, 39);
CapacitiveSensor   cs_10_41 =
CapacitiveSensor(10, 41);
CapacitiveSensor   cs_10_43 =
CapacitiveSensor(10, 43);
CapacitiveSensor   cs_10_45 =
CapacitiveSensor(10, 45);
CapacitiveSensor   cs_11_47 =
CapacitiveSensor(11, 47);

int note[noteCount] = {
  0, 1, 2, 3, 4, 5, 6, 7, 8, 9, 10, 11, 12, 13,
  14, 15, 16, 17, 18, 19, 20, 21, 22, 23, 24,
25, 26, 27, 28, 29, 30, 31, 32, 33, 34, 35, 36
};

int ThresholdOn = 500;
int ThresholdOff = 50;
int MIDIchannel = 1;
int startNote = 36; // Note C2
int Flag[noteCount];
int decayFlag[noteCount];
long total[noteCount];
int n, x;
unsigned long noteStartTime[noteCount];
unsigned long decayTime = 2000; // 2000 ms
```

```
//--------------------------------------------
--

void setup()
{
  MIDI.begin(MIDI_CHANNEL_OMNI);
  MIDI.turnThruOn();

  for (x = 0; x < noteCount; x++) {
    Flag[noteCount] = 0;
    decayFlag[noteCount] = 0;
  }

  MIDI.sendProgramChange(programChangeNum,
MIDIchannel);
}

//-------------------------------------

void loop()
{

  total[0] = cs_2_54.capacitiveSensor(20);
  total[1] = cs_2_55.capacitiveSensor(20);
  total[2] = cs_2_56.capacitiveSensor(20);
  total[3] = cs_2_57.capacitiveSensor(20);
  total[4] = cs_3_58.capacitiveSensor(20);
  total[5] = cs_3_59.capacitiveSensor(20);
  total[6] = cs_3_60.capacitiveSensor(20);
  total[7] = cs_3_61.capacitiveSensor(20);
  total[8] = cs_4_22.capacitiveSensor(20);
  total[9] = cs_4_24.capacitiveSensor(20);
  total[10] = cs_4_26.capacitiveSensor(20);
  total[11] = cs_4_28.capacitiveSensor(20);
  total[12] = cs_5_30.capacitiveSensor(20);
  total[13] = cs_5_32.capacitiveSensor(20);
  total[14] = cs_5_34.capacitiveSensor(20);
  total[15] = cs_5_36.capacitiveSensor(20);
  total[16] = cs_6_38.capacitiveSensor(20);
  total[17] = cs_6_40.capacitiveSensor(20);
  total[18] = cs_6_42.capacitiveSensor(20);
  total[19] = cs_6_44.capacitiveSensor(20);
```

```
total[20] = cs_7_46.capacitiveSensor(20);
total[21] = cs_7_48.capacitiveSensor(20);
total[22] = cs_7_50.capacitiveSensor(20);
total[23] = cs_7_52.capacitiveSensor(20);
total[24] = cs_8_23.capacitiveSensor(20);
total[25] = cs_8_25.capacitiveSensor(20);
total[26] = cs_8_27.capacitiveSensor(20);
total[27] = cs_8_29.capacitiveSensor(20);
total[28] = cs_9_31.capacitiveSensor(20);
total[29] = cs_9_33.capacitiveSensor(20);
total[30] = cs_9_35.capacitiveSensor(20);
total[31] = cs_9_37.capacitiveSensor(20);
total[32] = cs_10_39.capacitiveSensor(20);
total[33] = cs_10_41.capacitiveSensor(20);
total[34] = cs_10_43.capacitiveSensor(20);
total[35] = cs_10_45.capacitiveSensor(20);
total[36] = cs_11_47.capacitiveSensor(20);


for (n = 0; n < noteCount; n++) {

   if ((total[n] >= ThresholdOn) && (Flag[n]
== LOW)) {
      MIDI.sendNoteOn(note[n] + startNote, 100,
MIDIchannel); // Send a Note (pitch, velocity
100 on MIDI channel )
      noteStartTime[n] = millis();
      Flag[n] = HIGH;
      decayFlag[n] = HIGH;
   }


   if ((total[n] < ThresholdOff) && (Flag[n]
== HIGH)) {
      Flag[n] = LOW;
   }


   if (( millis() - noteStartTime[n] >=
decayTime) && (decayFlag[n] == HIGH)) {
      MIDI.sendNoteOff(note[n] + startNote,
100, MIDIchannel);
      Flag[n] = LOW;
      decayFlag[n] = LOW;
   }
```

```
    }
}
//----------------------------------
```

Listing 17: Source code for Encoder 1 for 5 Octave MIDI Touch Marimba

20.5 Source code for the 5 Octave MIDI Touch Marimba Encoder 2

```
/*
General MIDI Program Change percussion:
0x08 8 Celesta
0x09  9 Glockenspiel
0x0A  10  Music box
0x0B  11  Vibraphone
0x0C  12  Marimba
0x0D  13  Xylophone
0x0E  14  Tubular bell
0x0F  15  Dulcimer
*/

#include <CapacitiveSensor.h>
#include <MIDI.h>

MIDI_CREATE_DEFAULT_INSTANCE();

#define noteCount 24  // number of notes used
in the note range
#define programChangeNum 12  // Marimba

CapacitiveSensor    cs_2_54 =
CapacitiveSensor(2, 54);
CapacitiveSensor    cs_2_55 =
CapacitiveSensor(2, 55);
CapacitiveSensor    cs_2_56 =
CapacitiveSensor(2, 56);
CapacitiveSensor    cs_2_57 =
CapacitiveSensor(2, 57);
```

```
CapacitiveSensor    cs_3_58 =
CapacitiveSensor(3, 58);
CapacitiveSensor    cs_3_59 =
CapacitiveSensor(3, 59);
CapacitiveSensor    cs_3_60 =
CapacitiveSensor(3, 60);
CapacitiveSensor    cs_3_61 =
CapacitiveSensor(3, 61);
CapacitiveSensor    cs_4_22 =
CapacitiveSensor(4, 22);
CapacitiveSensor    cs_4_24 =
CapacitiveSensor(4, 24);
CapacitiveSensor    cs_4_26 =
CapacitiveSensor(4, 26);
CapacitiveSensor    cs_4_28 =
CapacitiveSensor(4, 28);
CapacitiveSensor    cs_5_30 =
CapacitiveSensor(5, 30);
CapacitiveSensor    cs_5_32 =
CapacitiveSensor(5, 32);
CapacitiveSensor    cs_5_34 =
CapacitiveSensor(5, 34);
CapacitiveSensor    cs_5_36 =
CapacitiveSensor(5, 36);
CapacitiveSensor    cs_6_38 =
CapacitiveSensor(6, 38);
CapacitiveSensor    cs_6_40 =
CapacitiveSensor(6, 40);
CapacitiveSensor    cs_6_42 =
CapacitiveSensor(6, 42);
CapacitiveSensor    cs_6_44 =
CapacitiveSensor(6, 44);
CapacitiveSensor    cs_7_46 =
CapacitiveSensor(7, 46);
CapacitiveSensor    cs_7_48 =
CapacitiveSensor(7, 48);
CapacitiveSensor    cs_7_50 =
CapacitiveSensor(7, 50);
CapacitiveSensor    cs_7_52 =
CapacitiveSensor(7, 52);

int note[noteCount] = {
  0, 1, 2, 3, 4, 5, 6, 7, 8, 9, 10, 11, 12, 13,
```

```
    14, 15, 16, 17, 18, 19, 20, 21, 22, 23
};

int ThresholdOn = 500;
int ThresholdOff = 50;
int MIDIchannel = 1;
int startNote = 73; // Note C#
int Flag[noteCount];
int decayFlag[noteCount];
long total[noteCount];
int n, x;
unsigned long noteStartTime[noteCount];
unsigned long decayTime = 2000; // 2000 ms

//-------------------------------------------------
--

void setup()
{
  MIDI.begin(MIDI_CHANNEL_OMNI);
  MIDI.turnThruOn();

  for (x = 0; x < noteCount; x++) {
    Flag[noteCount] = 0;
    decayFlag[noteCount] = 0;
  }

  MIDI.sendProgramChange(programChangeNum,
MIDIchannel);
}

//----------------------------------------

void loop()
{
 MIDI.read(); // Read the incoming MIDI

  total[0] = cs_2_54.capacitiveSensor(20);
  total[1] = cs_2_55.capacitiveSensor(20);
  total[2] = cs_2_56.capacitiveSensor(20);
  total[3] = cs_2_57.capacitiveSensor(20);
  total[4] = cs_3_58.capacitiveSensor(20);
  total[5] = cs_3_59.capacitiveSensor(20);
```

```
total[6] = cs_3_60.capacitiveSensor(20);
total[7] = cs_3_61.capacitiveSensor(20);
total[8] = cs_4_22.capacitiveSensor(20);
total[9] = cs_4_24.capacitiveSensor(20);
total[10] = cs_4_26.capacitiveSensor(20);
total[11] = cs_4_28.capacitiveSensor(20);
total[12] = cs_5_30.capacitiveSensor(20);
total[13] = cs_5_32.capacitiveSensor(20);
total[14] = cs_5_34.capacitiveSensor(20);
total[15] = cs_5_36.capacitiveSensor(20);
total[16] = cs_6_38.capacitiveSensor(20);
total[17] = cs_6_40.capacitiveSensor(20);
total[18] = cs_6_42.capacitiveSensor(20);
total[19] = cs_6_44.capacitiveSensor(20);
total[20] = cs_7_46.capacitiveSensor(20);
total[21] = cs_7_48.capacitiveSensor(20);
total[22] = cs_7_50.capacitiveSensor(20);
total[23] = cs_7_52.capacitiveSensor(20);

for (n = 0; n < noteCount; n++) {

    if ((total[n] >= ThresholdOn) && (Flag[n]
== LOW)) {
      MIDI.sendNoteOn(note[n] + startNote, 100,
MIDIchannel); // Send a Note (pitch, velocity
100 on MIDI channel )
      noteStartTime[n] = millis();
      Flag[n] = HIGH;
      decayFlag[n] = HIGH;
    }

    if ((total[n] < ThresholdOff) && (Flag[n]
== HIGH)) {
      Flag[n] = LOW;
    }

    if (( millis() - noteStartTime[n] >=
decayTime) && (decayFlag[n] == HIGH)) {
      MIDI.sendNoteOff(note[n] + startNote,
100, MIDIchannel);
      Flag[n] = LOW;
      decayFlag[n] = LOW;
    }
```

```
    }
}
//---------------------------------
```

Listing 18: Source Code for Encoder 2 for 5 Octave MIDI Touch Marimba

20.6 Explanation of the Source Code for Encoders 1 and 2

The source code for Encoders 1 and 2 is similar, but Encoder 1 has 37 touch switch inputs whereas Encoder 2 has only 24. Also Encoder 2 has a MIDI.Read() command in the main program Loop this enables MIDI commands from Board 1 Encoder to be passed through Board 2 and then to the common MIDI Out socket.

The Capacitive Sensor Library is called using:

```
#include <CapacitiveSensor.h>
```

The source code uses the MIDI Library:

```
//https://www.arduino.cc/reference/en/libraries/midi-library/

#include <MIDI.h>
MIDI_CREATE_DEFAULT_INSTANCE();
```

MIDI commands are initialized by:

```
  MIDI.begin(MIDI_CHANNEL_OMNI);
```

The noteCount for Board 1 is set to 37 and the Program Change number is set to 12 which is the Marimba:

```
#define noteCount 37  // number of notes used in
the note range
```

```
#define programChangeNum 12   // Marimba
```

The noteCount for Board 2 is set to 24 and the Program Change number is set to 12 which is the Marimba:

```
#define noteCount 24   // number of notes used in
the note range
#define programChangeNum 12   // Marimba
```

Board 1 and Board 2 touch switches are both initialized with the starting line:

```
CapacitiveSensor    cs_2_54 = CapacitiveSensor(2,
54);
```

The Variables and Constants for Board 1 are initialized with:

```
int note[noteCount] = {
   0, 1, 2, 3, 4, 5, 6, 7, 8, 9, 10, 11, 12, 13,
   14, 15, 16, 17, 18, 19, 20, 21, 22, 23, 24, 25,
26, 27, 28, 29, 30, 31, 32, 33, 34, 35, 36
};

int ThresholdOn = 500;
int ThresholdOff = 50;
int MIDIchannel = 1;
int startNote = 53; // Note F3
int Flag[noteCount];
int decayFlag[noteCount];
long total[noteCount];
int n, x;
unsigned long noteStartTime[noteCount];
unsigned long decayTime = 2000; // 2000 ms
```

The Variables and Constants for Board 2 are initialized with:

```
int note[noteCount] = {
   0, 1, 2, 3, 4, 5, 6, 7, 8, 9, 10, 11, 12, 13,
   14, 15, 16, 17, 18, 19, 20, 21, 22, 23
};

int ThresholdOn = 500;
```

```
int ThresholdOff = 50;
int MIDIchannel = 1;
int startNote = 73; // Note C#
int Flag[noteCount];
int decayFlag[noteCount];
long total[noteCount];
int n, x;
unsigned long noteStartTime[noteCount];
unsigned long decayTime = 2000; // 2000 ms
```

The Setup routine for both boards initialises MIDI, clears the Flags and sends a MIDI Program Change command:

```
MIDI.begin(MIDI_CHANNEL_OMNI);
MIDI.turnThruOn();

for (x = 0; x < noteCount; x++) {
  Flag[noteCount] = 0;
}

MIDI.sendProgramChange(programChangeNum,
MIDIchannel);
```

The main Loop routine for Board 1 reads the 37 switches, and for Board 2 reads 24 switches, starting in each case with:

```
total[0] = cs_2_54.capacitiveSensor(20);
```

In the FOR Loop if the total[n] is greater or equal to the ThresholdOn AND the Flag[n] is LOW then a corresponding MIDI Note On is transmittted, the present time millis() is stored in noteStartTime[n], the Flag[n] is set HIGH and the decayFlag[n] is set HIGH:

```
for (n = 0; n < noteCount; n++) {

  if ((total[n] >= ThresholdOn) && (Flag[n] ==
LOW)) {
    MIDI.sendNoteOn(note[n] + startNote, 100,
MIDIchannel); // Send a Note (pitch, velocity 100
```

```
on MIDI channel )
    noteStartTime[n] = millis();
    Flag[n] = HIGH;
    decayFlag[n] = HIGH;
  }
```

Also in the FOR Loop if the total[n] is less than the ThresholdOff AND the Flag[n] is HIGH then a corresponding MIDI Note Off is transmittted, and the Flag[n] is set LOW:

```
    if ((total[n] < ThresholdOff) && (Flag[n] ==
HIGH)) {
      Flag[n] = LOW;
    }

    if (( millis() - noteStartTime[n] >=
decayTime) && (decayFlag[n] == HIGH)) {
      MIDI.sendNoteOff(note[n] + startNote, 100,
MIDIchannel);
      Flag[n] = LOW;
      decayFlag[n] = LOW;
    }
  }
}
```

20.7 Circuit schematic diagram for Board 1 for the 5 Octave MIDI Touch Marimba Encoder

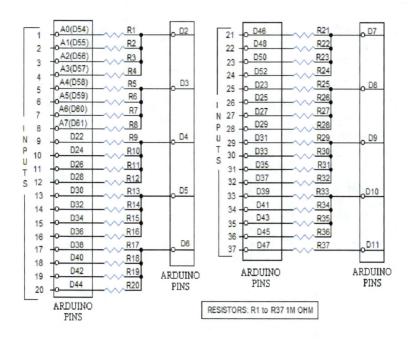

Figure 48: Circuit Schematic for Board 1 for a 5 Octave MIDI Marimba

20.8 Circuit schematic diagram for Board 2 for the 5 Octave MIDI Touch Marimba Encoder

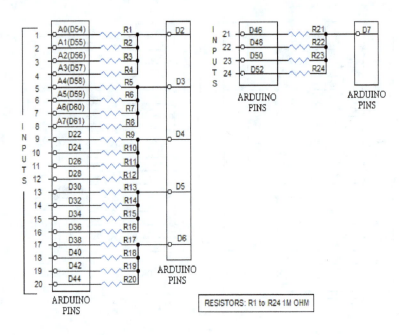

Figure 49: Circuit Schematic Board 2 MIDI Touch Marimba

20.9 Combining two 37 Note MIDI Touch Controller Boards

The +5 Volt (5V) and Ground (GND) pins are looped and connected to both boards. The serial TXO pin from board 1 is connected to the RXO pin of board 2. The TXO pin from board 2 is connected to PIN 5 of the MIDI Out socket via a 220 ohm resistor. Pin 4 of the MIDI Out socket is connected to +5 Volt via a 220 ohm resistor. Both boards can be powered via a single 9 Volt DC external power supply or via a singe USB connection. Note only one of the boards needs to be externally powered because the +5 Volt (5V) and the Ground (GND) pins are connected to each other.

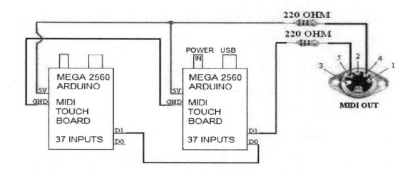

Figure 50: Combining two 37 Note MIDI Touch Controller Boards

20.10 MIDI Out Circuit Schematic diagram for 5 Octave Marimba

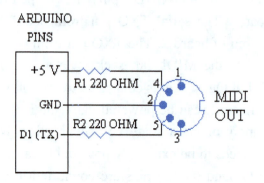

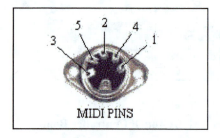

Figure 51: MIDI Out for 5 Octave Marimba

20.11 The 5 Octave Marimba Touch MIDI Out Wiring

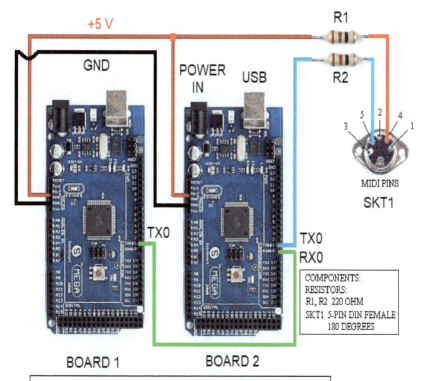

Figure 52: A 5 Octave Marimba Touch MIDI Out Wiring

The +5 Volt and Ground (GND) pins are looped and connected to both boards. The serial TX0 pin from board 1 is connected to the RX0 pin of board 2. The TX0 pin from board 2 is connected to PIN 5 of the MIDI Out socket via a 220 ohm resistor. Pin 4 of the MIDI Out socket is connected to +5 Volt via a 220 ohm resistor. Both boards can be powered via a single 9 Volt DC external power supply or via a single USB connection.

COMPONENTS:
RESISTORS:
R1, R2 220 OHM
SKT1 5-PIN DIN FEMALE
180 DEGREES

About the Author

Tom Scarff, founder of MIDI Music Kits, has been working in the Electronics Industry for more than 40 years. He spent nearly 15 years working in electronic maintenance, design and development in the Irish national broadcasting organisation, RTE. More recently he has been employed in the Dublin Institute of Technology, DIT (now the Technological University of Dublin, TUD) lecturing in Computer and Electronic Engineering and in Music Technology. He has also published a number of articles on topics including audio, music and MIDI in particular.

He has designed and produced a number of MIDI circuit designs using the ATmega series of micro-controllers. The designs are based on the Arduino and are compatible with the open-source IDE, which can be downloaded for free (currently for Mac OS X, Windows, and Linux).

He has spent many years working in the development and design of electronic music, building many different types of MIDI musical instruments. He saw how difficult it was to create simple MIDI instruments and he wanted to create something that makes it easier for people to create, build, connect and enjoy making their own musical instruments.

The author can be contacted via his website at:

https://www.midikits.net/